JOHN CALVIN

CASCADE COMPANIONS

The Christian theological tradition provides an embarrassment of riches: from scripture to modern scholarship, we are blessed with a vast and complex theological inheritance. And yet this feast of traditional riches is too frequently inaccessible to the general reader.

The Cascade Companions series addresses the challenge by publishing books that combine academic rigor with broad appeal and readability. They aim to introduce nonspecialist readers to that vital storehouse of authors, documents, themes, histories, arguments, and movements that comprise this heritage with brief yet compelling volumes.

TITLES IN THIS SERIES:

An Introduction to the Desert Fathers by Jason Byassee
Reading Paul by Michael J. Gorman
Theology and Culture by D. Stephen Long
Creation and Evolution by Tatha Wiley
Theological Interpretation of Scripture by Stephen Fowl
Reading Bonhoeffer by Geffrey B. Kelly
Justpeace Ethics by Jarem Sawatsky
Feminism and Christianity by Caryn D. Griswold
Angels, Worms, and Bogeys by Michelle A. Clifton-Soderstrom
Christianity and Politics by C. C. Pecknold
A Way to Scholasticism by Peter S. Dillard
Theological Theodicy by Daniel Castelo
The Letter to the Hebrews in Social-Scientific Perspective
    by David A. deSilva
Basil of Caesarea by Andrew Radde-Galwitz
A Guide to St. Symeon the New Theologian by Hannah Hunt
Reading John by Christopher W. Skinner
Forgiveness by Anthony Bash
The Rule of Faith by Everett Ferguson
Jacob Arminius by Rustin E. Brian
Jeremiah by Jack Lundbom
Richard Hooker by W. Bradford Littlejohn
Scripture's Knowing by Dru Johnson

JOHN CALVIN

A Companion to His Life and Theology

DONALD K. McKIM

 CASCADE *Books* • Eugene, Oregon

JOHN CALVIN
A Companion to His Life and Theology

Copyright © 2015 Donald K. McKim. All rights reserved. Except for brief quotations in critical publications or reviews, no part of this book may be reproduced in any manner without prior written permission from the publisher. Write: Permissions, Wipf and Stock Publishers, 199 W. 8th Ave., Suite 3, Eugene, OR 97401.

From *Calvin: Institutes*, (Library of Christian Classics) edited by John T. McNeill, © 1960. Used by kind permission of Westminster John Knox Press (www.wjkbooks.com).

Cascade Books
An Imprint of Wipf and Stock Publishers
199 W. 8th Ave., Suite 3
Eugene, OR 97401

www.wipfandstock.com

ISBN 13: 978-1-62564-760-3

Cataloguing-in-Publication Data

McKim, Donald K.

John calvin: a companion to his life and theology

Cascade Companions 25

166 + xii p. ; 23 cm. Includes bibliographical references.

ISBN 13: 978-1-62564-760-3

1. John Calvin 2. Title 3. Series

BX9421 .M45 2015

Manufactured in the U.S.A.   10/26/2015

To my wonderful family, with deepest gratitude

LindaJo, *my incomparably loving wife*

And our sons and families, who bring us great joy
    Stephen, Caroline, Maddie, and Annie McKim
    Karl and Lauren McKim

CONTENTS

Preface • ix

PART I LIFE OF CALVIN

1 Early Years and Education (1509–1536) • 3
2 Called to Geneva (1536–1538) • 21
3 Strasbourg (1538–1541) • 29
4 Return to Geneva (1541–1549) • 36
5 The Genevan Church (1550–1555) • 46
6 Final Years (1556–1564) • 52

PART II THEOLOGY OF CALVIN

7 Book I • 61
The Knowledge of God the Creator

8 Book II • 83
The Knowledge of God the Redeemer in Christ

9 Book III • 111
The Way in Which We Receive the Grace of Christ: What Benefits Come to Us from It, and What Effects Follow

10 Book IV • 132
The External Means or Aids by Which God Invites Us Into the Society of Christ and Holds Us There

Discussion Questions • 153
Select Bibliography • 163

PREFACE

My interest in John Calvin (1509–1564) has been longstanding. It began in high school through discussions with my pastor, Rev. John E. Karnes. I got my first copy of Calvin's *Institutes* on July 26, 1968. I studied Calvin through my years at Westminster College in New Wilmington, Pennsylvania, particularly in two years of rich independent study with Dr. Jack Rogers. Time at Pittsburgh Theological Seminary with the preeminent Calvin scholar, Ford Lewis Battles, added unsurpassable new dimensions to my appreciation of Calvin. Other seminary professors, Arthur Cochrane, John Gerstner, and Robert S. Paul also provided enriching perspectives. To all these teachers, I am deeply grateful.

Through my years of seminary teaching, work as an editor, and minister in the Presbyterian Church (USA), I have lectured and taught, written articles and papers, as well as written and edited books on Calvin. So it was a pleasure to be asked by Christian Amondson of Wipf & Stock Publishers to provide a self-contained introductory course for first year theology students or informed and interested laity on Calvin. My desires to introduce people to Calvin are always strong. So I appreciate this opportunity and doing this book was a labor of love.

These efforts are lovingly dedicated to my family. My wife LindaJo has loved me through forty years of marriage, for which no words or actions can express adequate thanks. This book is especially for her. Our son Stephen with his

Preface

wife, Caroline and their daughters, Maddie and Annie are true joys in every way. Our son Karl and his wife, Lauren help us celebrate the delights of life. They all bless us.

There is a vast scholarly literature on Calvin as well as a number of excellent introductions to Calvin's life and thought. I have read Calvin scholars gratefully and learned from them. But I tried to write this book to be accessible, with a minimum of formal documentation from secondary sources. Part I discusses Calvin's life. I am indebted to a number of sources here, some of which are indicated in the footnotes.

The second part of the book is a study of Calvin's theology expressed in his *Institutes of the Christian Religion* (1559). This was Calvin's major theological work through the years. A full study of Calvin's theology also needs to include his other writings, particularly his biblical commentaries. But I believe this book provides a unique approach among introductory works on Calvin. Here is a narrative exposition of Calvin's thought as found in his 1559 *Institutes*, which other introductions to Calvin do not offer in this same way. I have wanted Calvin's voice to be heard, a sort of "back to the sources" (Lat. *Ad fontes!*) approach, which Calvin's training in Renaissance Humanism fostered within him. The goal is not only to say things *about* Calvin; but also to listen to words *from* Calvin. His own words are the best source. So I have tried to let Calvin speak and explain his meanings as much as possible.

I believe this approach presents some advantages for those initially approaching Calvin's life and thought. It enables levels of study.

First, the book can be read for an overview of Calvin's theology, following the path of the four Books of his *Institutes*. This allows one to get a sense of the structure of the *Institutes* overall, as well as the flavor and content

Preface

of Calvin's theological concerns and viewpoints. So read the book "as is" to gain a sense of the whole of Calvin's *Institutes*.

Second, the book can be read alongside the text of the *Institutes* itself. Quotations in the present book are drawn from the *Institutes*. There they can be read in their larger contexts along with the other things Calvin has to say that are not covered here. One can also find the supports he offers in his book for the quotations cited here. So this book can open into a more careful and detailed study of Calvin's text itself. The narrative here tries to highlight important elements of Calvin's understanding of the theological topics he considers. This book does not present every portion of the *Institutes*. But it does try to discuss the main theological issues that engaged Calvin in his book through the years. So let this book open windows to further, more thorough Calvin study.

References to the *Institutes* are given in book, chapter, section notation. So 3.20.2 is Book 3, chapter 20, section 2. Quotations following these references are from the same section, until a new reference notation is given. The *Institutes* text used is the translation of Ford Lewis Battles in the Library of Christian Classics series (see the Select Bibliography).

The Discussion Questions provide opportunities for reflection and conversations about the substance of Calvin's viewpoints. They open us to ways of enhancing our learning as we probe the topics and dialogue with others.

My hope is that this book can help readers understand Calvin's life and theology. May it also be an impetus to more sustained study of this preeminent theologian. Resources in the Select Bibliography provide ways of engaging more fully with Calvin literature. Beyond items listed there, a large array of specialized studies on topics in Calvin's thought awaits inquiry.

So this book introduces us to John Calvin, his life and theology. For him, theological reflection engaged the whole person in coming to a knowledge of God and God's revelation in Jesus Christ. For Calvin, seeking to understand the Christian faith is an ongoing task and joy for Christians. His theological work was meant to help those whose faith leads them to seek further understanding, an understanding of mind and heart which bursts into the praise and service of God. As Calvin said in his 1538 *Catechism*: "We are to conceive the Christian faith as no bare knowledge of God or understanding of Scripture which rattles around the brain and affects the heart not at all . . . But it is a firm and staunch confidence of the heart by which we securely repose in God's mercy promised us through the Gospel."[1]

Donald K. McKim
Germantown, Tennessee
Easter 2015

---

1. *John Calvin: Catechism 1538*, 17–18.

PART I
LIFE OF CALVIN

1

EARLY YEARS AND EDUCATION (1509-1536)

JOHN CALVIN WAS THE son of Gerhard Calvin, a lawyer and an administrative official for the cathedral church in Noyon, France, located in Picardy, some sixty miles northeast of Paris. Calvin was born on July 10, 1509. His mother, Jeanne Le Franc, who was noted for her piety, died around 1515. The family consisted of several brothers, some of whom died early in life. Two sisters completed the household, which later also included a stepmother and stepsisters.

Gerhard was able to secure a benefice or scholarship from the cathedral to help finance education for his young son. Calvin kept the benefice until 1534 when he resigned it during the time he was aligning himself with the emerging Protestant movement. In the course of his educational journeys, three universities and six teachers played significant roles.

When he was fourteen, John Calvin traveled from Noyon to attend the University of Paris. He intended to fulfill his father's wishes to become a priest in the Roman Catholic Church. Calvin probably enrolled in the Collège de la Marche of the university in 1523, where he studied with the Latin scholar, Mathurin Cordier.

After three months, Calvin transferred to the Collège de Montaigu where he studied what now would be called the liberal arts. This prepared students for later study in law or theology. This college, where the famous Erasmus had been a student, was known for its strict academic atmosphere and deplorable living conditions for students. Yet Calvin persevered and, in 1527, finished his degree.

But a change of plans intervened. Gerard Calvin came into dispute with the Noyon cathedral officials and was excommunicated from the church. This humiliating turn of events led John's father to determine that his son should not pursue a vocation in the church as a priest, but should switch to the study of law. This would avoid church associations and be a more lucrative life for young John.

Obediently, in late 1527 or early 1528, John moved from Paris to Orléans, the preeminent center in France for the study of law. Since the ninth century, law had been taught in this university and Law was its only faculty. Five professors taught civil law; and three taught canon (church) law. Here Calvin became acquainted with emerging methods of legal research that were to be important in his later life as a theologian. The "modern" school was developing important textual, linguistic, and historical materials relating to Justinian's *Corpus Juris Civilis*, the historical commentary on ancient Roman laws. The traditional way of analyzing ancient texts was philosophically—through the categories of late medieval thought and Aristotelian logic. The developing movement called humanism reoriented the study of texts to stress elements such as the language of the text, its historical backgrounds and contexts, as well as ways texts were understood through rhetoric, and how texts were used by those who read them.

The methods of Renaissance humanism that Calvin learned in studying law at Orléans were important for his

Early Years and Education (1509–1536)

later approach to biblical interpretation and the study of Christian theology. In his sixteenth-century context, Calvin encountered Renaissance humanism as a way of thinking and a literary and scholarly approach to what today we call the "humanities." It was not in itself either pro- or antireligious. Humanists valued ancient authorities more than contemporary ones and emphasized learning the languages of antiquity and returning to the ancient texts of the Greeks and Romans. The motto: *Ad fontes!* ("To the Sources!") captured this approach of focusing on the "fount" or ancient springs of knowledge and wisdom to renew what had been lost through the centuries by layers of opinions that scholars had added to the ancients.

The movement of "Christian humanism" focused on the Christian faith. Christian humanists wanted to recover the wisdom of ancient Christianity by asking what Christ and the apostles had taught and what true Christianity should be like. This led to an emphasis on study of the Bible, the "source document" of Christian faith. Christian humanists wanted to approach the study of Christianity historically, studying the biblical languages, culture, and understanding what church theologians taught during the early church period. Their emphasis was on linguistic, literary, historical study rather than approaching ancient texts through the categories of logic and dialectics that had developed into technical disciplines during the previous centuries. For Christian humanists, biblical texts should be interpreted in light of their contexts, their backgrounds, and the intentions with which they were written. Attention to rhetorical dimensions meant emphasizing the persuasive power of texts to convey effective truth to hearers. Leading Christian humanists included Desiderius Erasmus (1469–1536), Lefèvre d'Etaples (1455?–1536), Gulielmus Budaeus (Budé—1467–1540), and Juan Vives (1492–1540).

Calvin's most influential humanist teacher was Budé who instructed him in legal terms, literature, political philosophy, and Roman institutions. The method of Calvin's first major publication, his *Commentary on Seneca's "De Clementia,"* owed much to Budé's work. Budé opened Calvin to the importance of a range of disciplines for helping him understand life and interpret texts. These were insights Calvin later put to good use in interpreting the Scriptures.

In 1529, Calvin was attracted to the University of Bourges where the Italian jurist Andreas Alciati had begun to lecture. Alciati's reputation was as a lawyer who used Justinian's *Corpus* to tackle contemporary problems. At the same time, he viewed Roman law within the larger setting of its place in the history of Latin language, literature, and history while applying textual criticism to the study of law. In this way, Alciati brought the new humanist approach to law study. The jurist's bombastic style was off-putting to Calvin but he appreciated Alciati's critical approach and emphases on historical contexts.

After two years at Bourges (1529–1531), Calvin returned to Paris to study literature for a year (1531–1532), and then finished his law degree at Orléans (1532–1533).

Calvin's return to Paris was occasioned by the death of his father on May 26, 1531. Since Gerard had not been reconciled to the church, he was not eligible to receive the church's sacraments. John's brother, Charles, was able to arrange for a posthumous absolution for their father so he could be buried in consecrated ground. But without his father's instruction to study law, John returned to the University of Paris to imbibe humanist emphases, study Greek and perhaps Hebrew, and prepare himself for a life of scholarship.

A plague broke out in the Fall of 1531 and Calvin moved back to Orléans. He completed his *Commentary on*

Early Years and Education (1509–1536)

Seneca's "De Clementia" in February 1532. This was to be Calvin's first venture into humanist scholarship, a project that focused on Seneca (4 BCE–65 CE), a Roman statesman and philosopher. Seneca's book was written late in his life, after he had been an advisor to the emperor Nero. The book dealt with the nature of power and justice, giving instruction to a ruler who did not want to be a tyrant. Calvin's goal was to improve on the edition of Seneca's work produced by the great Erasmus in 1529 and also to display his scholarly skills in law, language, and philosophy. His approach was to follow Seneca's text, line by line seeking to indicate what was in the mind of the author.[1]

Calvin's commitment to this method was displayed throughout his later work as a biblical commentator where he approached biblical texts in the same way. Since Calvin's attempt to secure a patron to help with the financial burden of publishing the work failed, he had to use his own funds and secure a loan to have the book printed. The stress of the work affected Calvin's health and he was afflicted with severe diarrhea. Calvin soon also became disappointed that his book did not bring scholarly acclaim to its young author.

Calvin's return to Orléans enabled him to complete his law degree, but, beyond that, we do not know much about what he did for a year and a half.

CONVERSION

A doctrine that Calvin was to emphasize throughout his life as a theologian was the doctrine of Providence. One aspect of providence is that God leads and guides our lives. It is a doctrine that is, perhaps, best recognized in retrospect—as one looks back at life, sees where one has been, and where

1. See Battles, trans., *Calvin's Commentary on Seneca's "De Clementia."*

one has been led. This was what Calvin experienced in his own life.

Unlike the Protestant reformer Martin Luther (1483–1546), who often expressed himself in very personal terms, Calvin was much more reticent. We do not know much about Calvin's life or biography from Calvin himself. One source, however, does give us some insight. In Calvin's Preface to his *Commentary on the Psalms*, he wrote this about his life path; and the role of God in preparing him for his life's work:

> From my early childhood
> My father had destined me
> For theology:
> But after a time,
> Having considered that the knowledge of the law
> Commonly enriches those who follow it,
> This hope suddenly made him change his mind.
> That was the reason
> I was withdrawn
> From the study of philosophy
> And put into the study of law,
> To which, although, in obedience to my father,
> I tried to apply myself faithfully.
> God nevertheless by his secret providence
> Finally made me turn
> In another direction.[2]

This "new direction" in Calvin's life is a reference to his view that "my whole past life had been steeped in ignorance and error" and that he was "so obstinately devoted to the superstitions of the Papacy that it was difficult to pull me

---

2. From Calvin's Preface to his *Commentary on the Psalms* (1555) in the "prose-poetic" translation of Ford Lewis Battles in *Institutes of the Christian Religion* (1536), xxix–xxx.

Early Years and Education (1509–1536)

out of that very deep morass."[3] As Calvin continued, "My mind which, despite my youth, had been too hardened in such matters," now "was readied for serious attention."

Then we have the intriguing statement: "By a sudden conversion God turned and brought it to docility."[4] The statement is of interest because we do not have a clear sense of what Calvin means here. Did he have a "Damascus-road experience" like New Testament Saul, persecutor of the church who, on the road to Damascus encountered the living Christ in a bright light (Acts 9:1–9) and was transformed—as "Paul" into Christianity's greatest early missionary? This would have meant a sudden, radical, reorientation of his life and values to be aligned with what Calvin was to go on to recognize as the true gospel of Jesus Christ. Throughout Christian history, these kinds of experiences have happened to people. They are able to name the exact time and place where their "conversion" to Jesus Christ occurred.

If this dramatic type of experience did not happen to Calvin, perhaps he was alluding to what became a thorough emphasis throughout his developing theology: it is God who brings about our "conversion" and is the one who initiates and guides our lives of faith in Jesus Christ. God "turned" Calvin from the life of an aspiring humanist scholar to the life of a Christian theologian and pastor who devoted his life to the proclamation of the gospel. God brought his life into "docility" or "teachableness" as Calvin sought to understand and expound God's Word in Scripture. Calvin himself could claim no credit for the "conversion" that happened to him. He recognized it all, fully, to be the work of

---

3. Quoted in Battles, ed. and trans., *Institutes* (1536), xxx.

4. Ibid., xxxii. The Latin phrase, *subito conversio*, can be translated "sudden conversion" or "unexpected turnabout." Cf. Elwood, *Calvin for Armchair Theologians*, 10.

God. Just as Calvin had seen God's "secret providence" in making him "turn in another direction" when he had been studying law, so he saw the work of God in bringing him to faith and "to betake myself into thy life."[5]

While we cannot know exactly what Calvin meant by his "sudden conversion" or his new entrance into the Christian life, we do know the outcomes.

BECOMING A PROTESTANT

Calvin's "turn" drew him into becoming a Protestant Reformer. His way into this new vocation was prepared by a number of factors. Calvin's humanist studies brought him into contact with a number of people who in addition to discussing humanist ideas were also discussing religious ideas of the German Augustinian monk, Martin Luther. Luther had kicked off what later came to be known as the Protestant Reformation with his criticisms of the Roman Catholic Church, scholastic theology, and specifically the practices of indulgences.

Luther's famous 95 *Theses* are said to have been posted on the church door at Wittenberg, Germany where Luther was a professor, on October 31, 1517. These theological affirmations questioned church practices and theology and were occasioned specifically by the efforts of the Roman Church to raise money for construction of St. Peter's church in Rome by selling indulgences. These were ways by which the deceased could have their time in purgatory shortened through the purchase of an "indulgence" by someone on their behalf. The monk Johann Tetzel was in charge of these sales in the Wittenberg area. As a popular rhyme put

---

5. Ibid., xxxiii. This phrase is from "Reply to Sadolet" and can also be translated "to accept thy life." *Calvin: Theological Treatises*, ed. Reid, 253.

Early Years and Education (1509–1536)

it: "When a coin in the coffer rings; a soul from purgatory springs." Luther rejected this practice as being unbiblical.

As tensions mounted, Luther was excommunicated from the Roman Catholic Church and went on to develop his theological understandings based on his understanding of Scripture as the authority for the church and his rejection of the authority of the Pope. Luther's theology emphasized salvation or justification by God's grace through faith alone. Persons are saved by faith in Jesus Christ, not by their participation in the sacraments of the Roman Church or by any "good works."

As the Reformation spread in Germany, similar theological ideas were being developed in Switzerland by Huldrych Zwingli (1484–1531) and other reformers. Prominent German and Swiss cities became allied with Luther's and Zwingli's influences, adopting the teachings of what became known as the Evangelical movement and "Protestantism." Their emphases were not toward creating a new church as much as reforming the current church, in light of what were believed to be the teachings of Holy Scripture. Critiques centered on church abuses such as buying and selling church offices, poor clergy performance of duties, and the holding of multiple church offices by single individuals. These practices were viewed as compromising the church's claim to be "the body of Christ." Reforming ideas led to breaks with the church of Rome and rejection of papal authority as its central feature.

Calvin's professor of Greek at Bourges, Melchior Wolmar, had entertained Lutheran ideas. By the time Calvin completed his legal studies he would have been familiar with Luther's thought. Just as it is not certain what Calvin meant by his "conversion," so it is also not certain "when" this occurred. If it were a gradual event, it likely took shape after the publication of his Seneca commentary in 1532 and during the year 1533.

We know that Calvin was in Paris in 1533, during a time when political and religious tumults were occurring. Calvin recounted this about the period after his "conversion":

> Having therefore received
> Some taste and knowledge
> Of true piety,
> I was suddenly fired
> With such a great desire to advance
> That, even though I had not forsaken
> The other studies entirely,
> I nonetheless worked at them
> More slackly.[6]

So we can assume that during the summer and fall of 1533, Calvin was studying—probably the early church theologians in an effort to go "back to the sources"—as well as lecturing on Seneca's *De Clementia* in Paris.

But again, events intervened. Calvin's good friend Nicholas Cop (c. 1501–1540) was installed as the rector of the University of Paris on All Saints Day, November 1, 1533. Cop, like Calvin, was a humanist and interested in promoting reforms at the university. His rectoral address was titled "Christian Philosophy." The address startled the audience because it sounded like the voice of Erasmus and, more troubling, also of Martin Luther. In particular, Luther's interpretation of Matthew 5:3 ("Blessed are the poor in spirit, for theirs is the kingdom of heaven") was cited at length. Due to the sophistication of Cop's comments about

---

6. Ibid., xxxiii from the Preface to Calvin's commentary on the Psalms.

the Law of God (Cop was a physician, not a theologian), theologians of the university suspected someone had helped or composed his address for him.

It has always been a question of whether or to what degree Calvin was or may have been involved with Cop's address. Calvin's successor and friend Theodore Beza's (1519–1605) biography of Calvin attributes the address to him. But a number of issues surround this question. A safe assessment is that Calvin would have been aware of Cop's views whether or not he actually wrote the address.[7]

What happened, however, was that Cop's address evoked a blaze of controversy from angry conservative leaders. Cop was dismissed and called before King Francis I, who despite earlier indications of support for humanists, was now determined to suppress any heresy. Cop fled to Basel. Calvin escaped just before his room was to be searched and left the city, disguised—a sign of the peril he felt.

Through the generosity of friends, Calvin was able to spend time in the south of France, studying in the libraries of his friend from student days, Louis du Tillet, a Claix priest. He visited with the dean of humanists, Lefèvre d'Etaples, at the court of Marguerite of Navarre, a patroness of humanists and a Protestant sympathizer as well as sister to King Francis I. We have no account of what transpired in the meeting between d'Etaples and Calvin. But Beza reported that "this good old man . . . was delighted with young Calvin, and predicted that he would prove a distinguished instrument in restoring the kingdom of heaven in France."[8]

---

7. A translation of Cop's address is in Battles, *Institutes* (1536), Appendix III. Battles notes that "while a final determination of the authorship of this document cannot be made here, our notes point out a number of significant parallels with Calvin's later writings," 363.

8. Beza, *The Life of John Calvin*, 12.

At this point, Calvin was a person without a church. There were no Protestant churches in France. Did Calvin continue to attend Mass? We don't know his activities in these days. There is some thought that, while staying with du Tillet, he began to write his *Institutes of the Christian Religion*, the first edition of which appeared in 1536 and in its later Latin and French editions was to become his most well-known and significant theological work.

In May 1534, Calvin returned to his hometown, Noyon, to resign his church benefices. This action apparently signaled a break with the Roman Catholic Church. Perhaps Calvin's "sudden conversion" had occurred by or around this time. Calvin would have to depend now on the generosity of friends to support himself and his scholarship. But he had apparently moved on in his theological understandings to where he could no longer continue to consider his views compatible with the Roman Catholic Church.

An event in Paris on October 17, 1534 was also to play a role in Calvin's developing religious faith. That night, tracts (placards) that denounced Roman Catholic "abuses" and the Mass as an abomination were placed around Paris and in other French cities. Nortoriously, a placard was posted on the door of the king's bedchamber! The "Affair of the Placards" was the work of a network of Protestant sympathizers. But the king was not amused. He was afraid this act was a sign of unrest to come so he acted quickly and brutally. Several hundred sympathizers of reform were rounded up, books were seized, and nine persons were executed. Another outbreak of placards, on January 9, 1535, led to even more violence with eleven executions, banishments, and seizure of goods.

After the first Affair, Calvin could see the writing on the wall and knew he needed to flee his native land. He thus became an exile, a pilgrim, now cut off from family and

Early Years and Education (1509–1536)

friends.[9] Calvin and his friend Louis du Tillet left France under assumed names—Calvin was Martinus Lucianus—and followed the Rhine to the Swiss city of Basel. Calvin wanted a quiet place to pursue his studies and writings.

Nearly a decade before, Basel had adopted the Reformation in 1525. It was a gathering place for humanists; Erasmus resided there in the 1520s and 1530s. While Calvin was in Orléans, he had begun writing his first theological work, *Psychopannychia*. This term means "soul sleep" and relates to the question of what happens to the soul after death and before the Last Judgment. That the soul "sleeps" during this period had been declared a heresy by the Fifth Lateran Council of the church in 1513. Calvin's treatise was to counter the heresy of soul sleep which had made a reappearance in the teachings of the emerging Anabaptist movement. Calvin had been in touch with the Protestant reformer Wolfgang Capito (1478–1541) in Strasbourg, who urged him not to publish it. Calvin didn't; and in Basel he rewrote the work with a new Foreword (1536). The work was not published until 1542.[10]

Calvin's work was written in part, it seems, to counter the teachings of Michael Servetus (1511?–1553), a Spanish humanist and medical doctor who was spreading a variety of theological ideas—a number of them heretical. Calvin had known Servetus from his student days in Paris and a meeting was arranged between the two men in Paris. Calvin wanted to persuade Servetus of his errors. But Servetus was a no-show, which Calvin remembered and mentioned a couple decades later at the time when Servetus was on trial in Geneva. But even more, this work showed Calvin's use of biblical texts and his growing sense of personally

---

9. The "pilgrim" image is developed by Selderhuis, *John Calvin: A Pilgrim's Life*.

10. See de Greef, *The Writings of John Calvin*, 151–53.

appropriating the biblical message as a story for his own life. Life's focus is on God alone. The journey of the pilgrim has anxieties, afflictions, and sufferings. But obedience to God pulls one forward. The promises of God are real and sustain throughout life and death.

Calvin found a number of humanist and Reformed-oriented friends in Basel, a city also made attractive by its printing industry. Among those with whom he got acquainted were Oswald Myconius (1488-1552) the successor to Johann Oecolampadius (1482-1531) as the primary reformer in the city and also Wolfgang Capito, a reforming minister in Strasbourg. Calvin also got to know Simon Grynaeus (1493-1541), who taught Greek in the city and to whom Calvin later dedicated his commentary on Romans; and Sebastian Münster (1488-1552), a professor of Hebrew in the University who edited a two-volume edition of the Hebrew Bible, published in Basel in 1534-1535. Nicolas Cop was also there. Important reformers with whom Calvin would have future associations were Pierre Viret (1511-1571) and Heinrich Bullinger (1504-1575), who succeeded Zwingli as the leading minister in Zurich.

1536 INSTITUTES

A most significant dimension of Calvin's time in Basel was in finishing and polishing what became the first edition of his greatest theological work, the *Institutes of the Christian Religion*. Though Calvin had never formally studied theology in an academic institution, his amazing output of significant theological works, beginning with the 1536 *Institutes*, is astonishing. Calvin had probably begun work on the *Institutes* while with du Tillet in France but continued working on it after he arrived in Basel at the end of

Early Years and Education (1509–1536)

1534. It was completed by September 10, 1535, though not published until March 1536.

The 1536 *Institutes* began as a catechism to provide an "elementary form of teaching" in the Christian faith. It identifies as "evangelical Christians" those who believed they were returning to the "evangel" or "gospel" (Gr. *evangelion*) of the New Testament, which tells of Jesus Christ. Calvin sought to ground what he wrote in biblical teaching so that the truth of the gospel could become plain.

An important feature of this work was its dedication. Calvin decided to present this theological work to the King of France, King Francis I. This dedicatory letter to the King remained the same and intact through all the editions of the *Institutes* to 1560. He cast it as presenting a confession of faith. He wanted to show that the faith being confessed by the persecuted evangelicals in France is the true Christian faith. The Letter functions as an "apology" in the classic sense of a reasoned defense of a point of view. Despite the errors of the Roman Catholic Church, which Calvin points out, and the charges the Church was leveling against the evangelicals, there is a true Christian faith to be found as one returns "to the sources" and hears the message of the Scriptures of the Old and New Testaments. Evangelicals were following the true faith taught in Scripture and in the catholic and apostolic church of ancient times.

Calvin wanted to show that the evangelicals who were being persecuted were not corrupting the church or threatening the established government. Roman Catholic writers equated the evangelicals with radical Anabaptists rebels. Instead, Calvin urged obedience of subjects to their lawful rulers: "We owe this attitude of reverence and therefore of piety toward all our rulers in the highest degree, whatever they may be like."[11] However, one caution

11. Battles, *Institutes* (1536), 224.

stood out. Obedience to a human ruler could not become disobedience to God. As Calvin put it at the end of the 1536 *Institutes*:

> But in that obedience which we have shown to be due the authority of rulers, we are always to make this exception, indeed, to observe it as primary, that such obedience is never to lead us away from obedience to him, to whose will the desires of all kings ought to be subject, to whose decrees their commands ought to yield, to who majesty their scepters ought to be submitted . . . The Lord, therefore, is the King of kings, who, when he has opened his sacred mouth, must alone be heard, before all and above all men, next to him we are subject to those men who are in authority over us, but only in him. If they command anything against him, let it go unesteemed.[12]

These perspectives were to have important influences for those who adhered to Calvin's teachings from the sixteenth century onward. While Christians are to be obedient to the state, they must draw the line when the state goes against the will of God. This can be seen as opening the door to resistance and certainly at points to the witness of churches against governments and their policies.

Calvin's 1536 *Institutes* began with a key statement that marked Calvin's theological approach through all subsequent editions: "Nearly the whole of sacred doctrine consists in these two parts: knowledge of God and of ourselves."[13] Knowledge of God and knowledge of ourselves

---

12. Ibid., 225. Cf. Calvin's 1559 *Institutes of the Christian Religion* 4.20.32 (ed. McNeill, trans. Battles). Unless indicated, references to the *Institutes* are to this translation and edition.

13. Ibid., 15.

Early Years and Education (1509–1536)

are intimately related. To know God, we must know who we are. We only truly know ourselves when we know who God is. What follows in the *Institutes* is the exploration of this perspective through all dimensions of Christian understanding. This means the study of theology—thought about God—is not a remote, detached, "academic" activity. It involves the one who is exploring theology in personal and practical ways. Theology is relational, involving God's relationship with us; and our relationship with God. Throughout the technical discussions of Christian theology that followed in Reformed theology—the tradition to which Calvin made significant contributions—this relational dimension has always needed to be kept in mind.

The first edition of the *Institutes* followed the design of Luther's 1529 *Small Catechism* in its structure. It consisted of six chapters: Law, Faith, Prayer, Sacraments, The Five False Sacraments, and Christian Freedom. These six chapters grew over the years to eighty chapters in the final Latin (1559) and French (1560) editions, as the structure also developed into four Books. Throughout, Calvin sought to base his theological understandings on the exegesis or interpretation of Scripture. He was later to write biblical commentaries on most books of Scripture. He saw the commentaries as providing the basics of scriptural teaching that were expressed more explicitly and systematically in the *Institutes*. Each type of work fed the other.

Calvin's commitment to Scripture study and the appropriation of the biblical message is seen in the Preface Calvin wrote to his cousin Robert Olivétan's French Bible (1535). One point Calvin made was that the Bible should be available to common people. He wrote: "But the ungodly voices of some are heard, shouting that it is a shameful thing to publish these divine mysteries among the simple common people." Calvin's answer was: "But since the Lord has chosen prophets for Himself from the ranks of shepherds, apostles from the boats of fishermen, why should He not even now deign to choose like disciples? . . . But I desire only this, that the faithful people be permitted to hear their God speaking and to learn from [God] teaching."[14]

During the time just prior to the publication of the *Institutes*, Calvin, using the pseudonym Charles d'Espeville (a name he had earlier used), traveled with his friend Louis du Tillet to Italy. He stayed in Ferrara for a few weeks at the court of the Duchess Renata, a daughter of King Louis XII of France who supported the reform. She was also the sister-in-law of King Francis I of France. In Ferrara, Calvin met refugees from France, including the French poet Clément Marot (1496–1544).

After returning to Basel, Calvin immediately set out for France under a temporary amnesty that had been established for refugees to return and renounce their heresies within the next six months. Calvin had things to put in order relative to his father's estate because he anticipated leaving France permanently. In Paris, he ordered his brothers to sell the family lands in Noyon and was joined by his brother Antoine and sister Marie, who were to come back to live with Calvin in Basel.

Calvin's plan, with his family members, was to go to Strasbourg, a city hospitable to evangelicals where he wanted to study and write in peace. But a war had broken out between Charles V of Germany and Francis I of France. Due to troop movements, the route to Strasbourg was closed. So the Calvin party had to go through the center of France and through the city of Geneva in Switzerland. There another "providential event" occurred that radically redirected Calvin's life into a totally new direction.

14. Ibid., 374. On Olivétan's Bible translation, see de Greef, *The Writings of John Calvin*, 70–74.

2

CALLED TO GENEVA (1536-1538)

UNLIKE CALVIN'S, COMMENTARY ON Seneca's *"De Clementia,"* Calvin's 1536 *Institutes* sold out quickly. In reform-minded areas, this catapulted Calvin to prominence as a new, strong, theological voice. Yet, he tells us that after he had left Basel, "wherever else I have gone, I have taken care to conceal that I was the author of that performance; and I had resolved to continue in the same privacy and obscurity."[1]

On their journey, the stay in Geneva was to last one night. No one knew in advance that Calvin would be lodging there. But his close friend, Louis du Tillet, found out that Calvin was in the city. Du Tillet excitedly informed the ministers of the city, including Guillaume (William) Farel (1489-1565) who had been a flaming evangelical reformer in Switzerland for several years and had been preaching for reform in Geneva since 1532. Earlier in 1536, Geneva had broken from its bishop and on May 21, 1536, the whole population of the city, led by Farel, took an oath to accept

---

1. Calvin, "Preface" to *Commentary on Psalms*, trans. James Anderson, Calvin Translation Society, 5 vols. (Edinburgh, 1845) 1:xlii.

the Reformation, "to live henceforward according to the gospel." Now the task was to reform the Genevan church.

The fiery Farel wasted no time in tracking down John Calvin, in the midst of this city of around ten thousand inhabitants. What followed was a dramatic confrontation, which can rightly be called one of the "hinges of history." Farel burst into Calvin's room and "detained me at Geneva, not so much by counsel and exhortation, as by a dreadful imprecation, which I felt to be as if God had from heaven laid his mighty hand upon me to arrest me."[2] Pulling out all the stops, according to Calvin, the red-headed Farel,

> who burned with an extraordinary zeal to advance the gospel, immediately strained every nerve to detain me. And after having learned that my heart was set upon devoting myself to private studies for which I wished to keep myself free from other pursuits, and finding that he gained nothing by entreaties, he proceeded to utter an imprecation that God would curse my retirement, and the tranquillity of the studies which I sought, if I should withdraw and refuse to give assistance, when the necessity was so urgent. By this imprecation I was so stricken with terror, that I desisted from the journey which I had undertaken; but sensible of my natural bashfulness and timidity, I would not bring myself under obligation to discharge any particular office.[3]

Wow! How stunned—and humbled—Calvin must have been. For him, there would be no more splendid isolation, cast away in an ivory tower to write his theology. Now the hand of God was upon him through Farel, who must

2. Calvin, Preface, 1:xlii.
3. Ibid., 1:xlii–xlviii.

Called to Geneva (1536-1538)

have seemed like an Old Testament prophet come back to life. Calvin felt compelled to answer the call of God to stay in Geneva and assist the Frenchman Farel with the work of reformation. Calvin was a person "under orders"—to obey the call of God and serve God in the church, in the midst of urban life in a city that would experience an influx of refugees, many from Calvin's own French homeland. Reluctantly, but obediently, Calvin said, "Yes."

What Calvin stepped into was a community at the very beginning of trying to find its way as a Protestant city. The Roman Catholic clergy of the city were expelled after the city decided to become Protestant. So there was a severe clergy shortage and not an organized, ecclesiastical structure in the city for regulating worship and the practical work of ongoing ministry.

Calvin did not feel equipped or prepared to be a "pastor" or "preacher." So he would accept only the title of "doctor" and "reader of the Holy Scriptures" to designate his responsibilities. As time went on, he evolved into many roles in Geneva. But his primary work at the start was to lecture on the Holy Scriptures. After a short trip to Basel to put things in order, Calvin began his work prior to September 5, 1536 by expounding the letters of Paul in Geneva's main church, Saint Pierre.

An indication of the brilliance of the new Geneva leader came in October 1536 at the public religious colloquy in Lausanne. There, ministers of the emerging Reformation were to discuss theology with representatives of the local Roman Catholic Church. Calvin became a leading voice for the Reformers and amazed the assembly by quoting the early church fathers—from memory!

In January 1537, Calvin was installed as a "Reader in Holy Scripture" by the City Council of Geneva. It was not the church but the civil authority that installed him to this position. Calvin participated in ministry in Geneva by joining with Farel in laying foundations for the Genevan church. On January 13, 1537, they presented a plan to the Council outlining steps to be taken to continue the Reformation in Geneva. The *Articles concernant l'organisation de l'eglise et due culte à Genève* (*Articles concerning the Organization of the Church and of Worship in Geneva*) featured four points: the monthly celebration of the Lord's Supper and keeping the Supper holy through the power of excommunication; singing the Psalms in worship; instruction for youth; and laws about marriage. Except for the frequency of celebrating the Lord's Supper, which the Council set at once quarterly, the Articles were approved. Calvin preferred a weekly celebration of the Supper, but the Council rejected this position, believing it might be too much for the people who in Roman Catholicism participated only once per year. Later Calvin was to arrange a staggered weekly celebration schedule among Genevan churches so one could find the Supper being celebrated every Sunday in one of the Geneva churches.

This plan for ordering the Genevan church was a supplement to a confession of faith Calvin and Farel had submitted on November 10, 1536. This was a "Confession of Faith which all the citizens and inhabitants of Geneva and the subjects of the country must promise to keep and hold."[4] The provision that all inhabitants had to sign the Confession meant that the process of doing so did not go smoothly.

This confession formed a basis for *Instruction in Faith* (1537; *Instruction et Confession de Foy*), a catechism in French drawn from Calvin's *Institutes* (1536). The catechism was positive in nature, seeking to explicate the teachings of Scripture in thirty-three sections. The next year, Calvin

---

4. See *Calvin: Theological Treatises*, 26–33.

published a Latin translation, titled *Catechism or Instruction of the Christian Religion of the Church of Geneva* (Basel, 1538), which gained the catechism a wider audience of readers interested in the Christian religion. Calvin said the translation was done "in order that the sincerity of that faith may be manifested also to other churches everywhere."[5] The Confession of Faith and the Catechism marked what Christians in Geneva were to believe.

CHURCH CONFLICT IN GENEVA

Things did not go smoothly for "that Frenchman," a disparaging term for Calvin used by some who did not appreciate all he was trying to do. The difficulties of getting everyone in the city to subscribe to the Confession of Faith was a sticking point. Even more, Pierre Caroli (1480–1550) charged Calvin with heresy, not teaching what was true to the Christian tradition. This related to views of whether or not Jesus Christ was fully God as the church taught for centuries. Caroli alleged Calvin was guilty of Arianism, a heresy named for Arius from the period of the early church. Arius taught that Jesus Christ was not fully God, but rather the first creature created by God. But if Jesus Christ were only a "creature," his death could not bring salvation or forgiveness of sin because it had no power to do so.

Meetings were held in Lausanne and Berne with Calvin making a major presentation. Both synods or church leaders' meetings unanimously voted to uphold Calvin and condemned Caroli's charges. Caroli was forced to flee

5. The translation from the French is found in Calvin, *Instruction in Faith (1537)*. This quotation is from Hesselink, *Calvin's First Catechism*, 1. Battles had earlier written that "the *Catechism* of 1537/38 represents a step in Calvin's long effort to translate his religious views into a practical pattern of Christian living." See *John Calvin: Catechism 1538*, iii.

to France and vacillated between Roman Catholicism and Protestantism. In 1540, Caroli accused Calvin and Farel of trying to block his attempts to become a Protestant minister. Calvin responded with a letter (August 10, 1540) and indicated he hoped to be reconciled with Caroli. But nothing happened.

The issue of bringing all Genevans to sign the Confession heated up and on November 12, 1537 the magistrates said all who would not sign the Confession would be banned. A tumultuous meeting on November 25 featured citizens accusing the city leaders of negating their freedom and trying to make them subservient to Farel and his circle. The ministers threatened to excommunicate those who would not confess the Confession. But on January 4, 1538, the Council of Two Hundred said no one could be kept away from participating in the Lord's Supper. This focused on the heart of the problem. Calvin and Farel believed the church should have spiritual jurisdiction and be helped by the government to carry it out. The city leaders did not want the ecclesiastical concerns to be the primary source of jurisdiction.

On February 3, 1538, new elections for city government were held and those elected were less favorable to Calvin and Farel. The issue of what instructions to follow for celebrating the Lord's Supper arose. This included whether unleavened bread should be used for the Easter worship service. The city of Berne, which held influence in Geneva, had prescribed this. At a synod (regional) meeting at the end of March 1538, the decision was for churches in the region to follow the practices of the church in Berne. For the Easter Sunday communion, unleavened bread should be used and it should not be broken.

The situation raised the question of authority in the church. Calvin and Farel were opposed to having church

Called to Geneva (1536–1538)

practices dictated by the civil authorities. Authorities in Geneva insisted that the practices of Berne be followed. Calvin and Farel said they would not use the Berne rites and would not serve the Lord's Supper to the whole city. On Easter Sunday, Calvin and Farel preached but refused to serve Communion. All three governing bodies in Geneva affirmed the Berne rites must be used. Calvin and Farel were deprived of their offices and ordered to leave the city within three days. The next day they were gone to Zurich.

Meetings of church leaders in Zurich led to support for Calvin but a reprimand for the way he handled the situation—an excess of zeal. The Genevan duo was seen as disturbing the unity of the Reformed church. Calvin and Farel maintained that while church ceremonies were negotiable, the ministers should have ecclesiastical jurisdiction on the matter of the bread in the communion. Attempts to have Calvin and Farel reinstated in Geneva were met with rejection by city officials. When Calvin attempted to come back to explain his proposals, he was turned away from the city. So the reformers were homeless.

Farel and Calvin next traveled to Basel. By July 1538, Farel had accepted a call to be pastor in Neuchâtel. Calvin spent time in Basel and Strasbourg. Calvin wrote, "I shall retire to Basle, waiting to understand what the Lord would have me to do."[6] He was looking for God's providential leading for the future. When he looked back at his Geneva experience, however, Calvin wrote:

> Above all, however, on looking back and considering the perplexities which surrounded me from the first time I went there [Geneva], there is nothing I dread more than returning to the charge from which I have been set free. For though when first I took it up I could discern the

6. *Letters of John Calvin*, 1:72.

calling of God which held me fast and by which I consoled myself, now, on the contrary, I am in fear that I would tempt him if I were to resume so great a burden, which I have already felt to be insupportable.[7]

To Calvin, it was inconceivable that he could—or would—return to Geneva, which had been the scene of failure, frustration, and heartbreak over trying to establish Christian faith in the churches.

---

7. The translation is from the fine biography, Gordon, *Calvin*, 84. Cf. *Letters of John Calvin*, 1:72.

3

STRASBOURG (1538-1541)

An invitation came. The leading reformer in Strasbourg, Martin Bucer (1491-1551), along with his colleague, Wolfgang Capito, invited Calvin to begin ministering to French refugees who had settled in the city and were forming a church congregation. Initially, Calvin was disinclined to go. He wanted to devote himself to his theological studies, especially to writing a second Latin edition of his *Institutes*. But as Farel had before him, Bucer invoked the image of Jonah fleeing from God and told Calvin that God would find him!

By September, Calvin had given in and began a three-year period as a pastor and teacher, which had important effects on him for the rest of his life. Calvin worked as a pastor to the French refugees and also lectured on theology in the Academy.

The Strasbourg Reformation was being shaped by Bucer who was establishing his independence from viewpoints of Luther in a number of areas. Liturgical reform was underway and on the issue of baptism, Bucer was establishing a position that varied from Luther and from the Anabaptist movement. The Anabaptists rejected infant baptism and said baptism should be administered only to adults who make a confession of Jesus Christ. But Bucer was a conciliatory figure. He worked tirelessly to try to bring reconciliation among the different Protestant parties, rejecting polemical stances in favor of trying to find ways of agreement. When Calvin arrived in the city, the emphasis of Bucer on church discipline was being enacted.

Calvin developed a deep friendship and admiration for Bucer, nearly a father-son relationship. Theologically and personally, Bucer's influences were significant for the thirty-year old theologian. Calvin influenced Bucer as well. During his time in Strasbourg, Calvin produced important theological works that helped establish his growing reputation and were significant in the developing Reformed theological tradition.

Calvin's duties with his congregation of around five-hundred persons were to preach and provide pastoral care. In 1539, he also began to teach New Testament interpretation at the local gymnasium, lecturing on the Gospel of John and also First Corinthians. Calvin preached twice each Sunday and was in charge of four services during the week. He used the liturgy of the Strasbourg church, which included the singing of the Psalms. In Geneva, Calvin had introduced this feature of Protestant worship. The issue of church discipline for those who wished to partake of the Lord's Supper did not become as problematic in Strasbourg where congregants had to present themselves to ministers to be examined. Bucer was not able to secure the church's sole right to excommunication. The city magistrates maintained control. But in this context, Calvin saw the need for flexibility when dealing with the civil authorities. Calvin became a citizen of Strasbourg on July 29, 1539 and received a steady salary from the city council.

Strasbourg (1538–1541)

Bucer, the vigorous reformer, sought church reform and also reform of Calvin's life. He sought a wife for his friend and presented a few candidates to Calvin, none of whom were suitable. In spring 1540, Jean Stordeur, an Anabaptist who under Calvin's influence had joined the Strasbourg congregation, died of the plague. On August 6, 1540, Calvin and Stordeur's widow, Idelette de Bure, were married. Farel officiated at the service. A son, Jacques, was born prematurely and died within a month. Perhaps other children were also born but none survived into childhood. After nearly nine years of marriage, Idelette died on March 29, 1549. Calvin was deeply saddened by the loss of his life's partner. He took Idelette's two children from her first marriage as his own. Later, when taunted by enemies for not having children, Calvin was able to say that he had thousands of children in many places, those who were following his theological understandings.

Key to Calvin's development during his time in Strasbourg was his growing understandings of liturgy and church music. Calvin followed the Strasbourg liturgy because he found it expressive of true worship. He also did not want his French congregation to cause disturbances with the greater Strasbourg church bodies. In preparation for an important Strasbourg musical book of Psalm tunes and texts, *Some Psalms and Songs Set to Music*, which appeared in 1539, Calvin prepared some Psalm versifications in French, using Strasbourg melodies. Some of the eighteen Psalms (with other texts) were prepared by Clément Marot, the famous French poet whom Calvin had earlier met and with whom he would later work in Geneva.[1] Psalms were considered the appropriate texts for congregational singing and Reformed churches in Geneva, Scotland, and other

---

1. A reproduction of the 1539 edition is available at https://archive.org/details/aulcunspseaulmes00delt.

places later were marked by the psalmody used by congregations in worship.

One of Calvin's most important achievements during his years in Strasbourg was the publication of a new and expanded edition of his *Institutes of the Christian Religion*. His 1539 *Institutes* now featured seventeen chapters instead of the six in the 1536 *Institutes*. Importantly, the 1539 *Institutes* featured a new organizational pattern with new topics such as free choice, election and predestination, justification by faith and grace alone, excommunication, and civil government. Now, said Calvin, he wanted to explore the theological *loci* (Lat. "places") or doctrines that emerged from the work of exegesis or biblical interpretation. This was important because it meant that Calvin could use his lectures (which later became commentaries) to treat matters of biblical interpretation from the biblical texts. What became his *Institutes of the Christian Religion* in a number of editions through the years, written in Latin and then translated into French, the vernacular of the people, treated theological matters in the form of doctrines or theological teachings.

The developing *Institutes* now became oriented to providing foundational and academic theological discussions rather than focused on catechetical or basic instruction and enhancing piety. The *Institutes* was now for students studying theology in preparation for Christian ministry serving the people of God in Christian churches. The *Institutes* would help them understand and rightly interpret the Word of God in Scripture. The *Institutes* was being built on biblical interpretation. In turn, this overall structure or framework, which came to embrace four "books" or discussions of God, Christ, Holy Spirit, and church, would help those who study Scripture gain a wide overview of what the

Strasbourg (1538–1541)

Bible teaches on these theological topics so they would have that in mind as they interpreted individual biblical texts.

Relatedly, Calvin's biblical commentary on the book of Romans appeared in 1540. In the Preface to this commentary on one of Paul's most important works, Calvin recalled to his friend Simon Grynaeus how three years prior "we had a friendly discussion about the best way of interpreting scripture." Then, "both of us felt that lucid brevity [Lat. *perspicua brevitas*] constituted the particular virtue of an interpreter." Further: "Since it is almost his only task to unfold the mind of the writer whom he has undertaken to expound, he misses his mark, or at least strays outside his limits, by the extent to which he leads his readers away from the meaning of his author."[2] So throughout his interpretation of Scripture, Calvin primarily sought to understand what the text meant to the biblical writer. This also meant Calvin was concerned most with the natural or literal sense of Scripture, while also using the tools and resources of the biblical humanists to help interpret biblical texts. In his commentaries, Calvin did not present long digressions on theological matters since these were covered in his *Institutes*.

Calvin's theological concerns as a pastor and theologian led him to deal with a matter of increasing concern among the emerging Protestant churches, the issue of the Lord's Supper. This was to prove to be the most divisive theological issue among the Protestants in the years to come. Those who followed Luther, Zwingli, and the Anabaptist movements all had distinctive views about the

---

2. Calvin, *Epistles of Paul The Apostle to the Romans and to the Thessalonians*, 1. See the discussion in Rogers and McKim, *The Authority and Interpretation of the Bible*, 114–16; and Gordon, *Calvin*, chap. 7: "'Lucid Brevity' for the Sake of the Church: Romans." Cf. McKim, ed., *Calvin and the Bible*.

nature of the Lord's Supper. Among the major questions was whether Jesus Christ is "present" in the Supper?

Calvin wrote his *Short Treatise on the Holy Supper of Our Lord and Only Saviour Jesus Christ* in French in 1540 and it was published the following year. In this work, Calvin laid out the origins of the controversies between Luther on one side and Zwingli and his associate Oecolampadius, on the other. Both these viewpoints, Calvin rejected. But he tried to find common ground and in later discussions with others, including Luther's friend Philip Melanchthon, Calvin wanted Protestants to be able to be reconciled on this divisive issue.

An important event of 1541 was the appearance of the first edition of Calvin's *Institutes* intended for a general audience and published in French. This event was significant for a number of reasons. The first was that it helped establish Calvin as a recognized founder of what became the modern French language. The book helped shape the French language to deal with questions of theology and morality. Second, the book was written in the vernacular of the people, instead of Latin, the language of the learned. Calvin wanted his work to be shared with ordinary Christians and not just with scholars. The emergence of a middle class of merchants and business persons who were not acquainted with Latin meant there was the need to address common persons in their own language. Calvin wrote for the people of his homeland, France, and for French-speaking Christians in the environs of Geneva. Calvin translated or paraphrased the Greek words of his Latin edition, omitted some classical references, and provided explanations and repetition of thought to help impress the content on a general audience. His use of familiar French expressions also made the book more accessible. In short, Calvin brought his theological thought into a form that was manageable to readers

Strasbourg (1538–1541)

who were not professional scholars or intellectuals. Surely Calvin's pastoral work with French speakers in Strasbourg fueled his desire to have his work available in the language of the people.[3]

Calvin's period in Strasbourg was important. The influence of Bucer, his pastoral work, and his theological writing established Calvin as a prominent theologian. Calvin participated in colloquys or discussions, in Worms and Regensburg. These were efforts to bring differing Protestant positions into a closer harmony. Though by nature shy and reserved, Calvin participated in these events not because he wanted to do so but because he believed God wanted him to do so. Yet, while he believed that, through the difficult circumstances in Geneva, God had called him to Strasbourg, Calvin did not give up his sense of hoping to help Geneva in the further establishment of the Reformation.

---

3. See the splendid English translation of this French edition by Elsie Anne McKee in Calvin, *Institutes of the Christian Religion: 1541 French Edition*.

4

RETURN TO GENEVA (1541-1549)

After the exile of Farel and Bucer, Roman Catholics within Geneva and outside Geneva sought to bring the city back to the Roman Catholic faith. What would happen in this regard was unclear.

Though Calvin had no thought of returning to Geneva, he did address a couple pastoral letters to the church there, urging that the unity of the church be upheld and that the people submit to the will of God. Calvin wanted the people to uphold the dignity of the office-bearers in the church and avoid schisms and sects that would tear the church apart.

Political tensions in Geneva were rising. A source of great pressure came when the city received a letter on March 18, 1539 from Cardinal Jacopo Sadoleto (1477–1547), bishop of Carpentras. This letter appealed to city leaders and the church of Geneva to return to the Roman church. The Cardinal urged the people not to turn their backs on centuries-old church traditions in favor of a recent religion, promulgated by Farel and Calvin, who were self-serving.

When Geneva's leaders realized that neither they nor local ministers had sufficient knowledge to answer the

Return to Geneva (1541–1549)

Cardinal, they turned to Calvin. The Strasbourg citizen received a copy of Sadoleto's letter and composed a response in six days in August. He refuted Cardinal Sadoleto's charges against the Reformation point by point. Calvin argued that the Protestant churches were not forsaking church tradition, but were returning to the true source of Christianity—Jesus Christ and the Scriptures that proclaimed him. Calvin and others were trying to renew the church, not destroy it. In his powerful theological defense, Calvin discussed the work of the Holy Spirit and the Word of God, justification by faith, and the church's sacraments. The "only true bond of ecclesiastical unity" said Calvin is in "Christ the Lord, who has reconciled us to God the Father."[1] Calvin's work was so powerful that Geneva did not in the future ever contemplate returning to the Roman Catholic Church.

Things were changing in Geneva. During Calvin's exile, those who had held political power had gone and the current leadership included those who had not opposed Calvin in his early days. So it was possible for them to reach out and ask for Calvin's help against Sadoleto. Political turmoil had continued after Calvin left. Some began to believe the city had made a mistake by banishing Farel and Calvin.

By September 1540, the Council decided to try to secure Calvin's return to Geneva. From a number of sides, Calvin was urged to return. Farel and Calvin's friend, Pierre Viret (1511–1571) mounted a campaign. But Calvin was not eager. He wrote: "I would rather die a hundred deaths than on that cross, on which I would daily perish a thousand times over."[2]

Then major Swiss churches began to weigh in on the matter. Zurich and Basel urged Strasbourg to permit Calvin to return, as the best way to stabilize the Genevan church

---

1. Calvin, "Reply to Sadolet," in *Calvin: Theological Treatises*, 256.
2. Cited in van't Spijker, *Calvin*, 65.

situation. These shows of support had an effect on Calvin. He decided to return.

His entrance to the city on September 13, 1541 was in stark contrast to the way he had left. This time he arrived with a mounted escort from the city. The city sent horses and a carriage to bring Idelette and the household belongings to Geneva where a house was being provided. Though Calvin had not foreseen or initially wanted this outcome, he wrote to Farel, "If it were up to me, I would rather do anything else than oblige you. But because I know that I do not belong to myself, I offer my heart to the Lord."[3]

ORGANIZING THE CHURCH

Right away, Calvin began to talk with the Council about how the church could be best organized. The *Draft Ecclesiastical Ordinances* were debated thoroughly and finally established on November 20, 1541. They functioned as the church's constitution. They provided for an ordered church that would carry out church discipline as needs arose. The church was to be governed by "four orders of office." These were: pastors, doctors, elders, and deacons. Each was to have specific responsibilities, all in the service of God in the ministries of the church. Pastors were to preach the Word of God and administer the sacraments. Doctors were charged with the instruction of church members and providing theological education for those preparing to become ministers. Elders were persons of the congregation who were to oversee the Christian lives of church members, carrying out church discipline and morality enforcement in cooperation with the pastors in a church court called the Consistory. Deacons were ministers to the poor and the sick, overseeing the hospital. They dispersed funds and

3. Cited in van't Spijker, *Calvin*, 65.

were concerned with the whole social welfare of those in need. The four offices in the church mirrored what Calvin had experienced in Strasbourg. Bucer wrote about the four offices in biblical commentaries on the Gospels and Paul's Letter to the Romans.

Not all Calvin's desires for structuring of the church were met. The Consistory was not granted full independence to administer church discipline. The weekly communion celebrations Calvin desired were rejected in favor of celebrating the Lord's Supper four times a year. Fearing the superstitions associated with the practice of the laying on of hands at a minister's ordination, the Council rejected Calvin's desire in this matter.

An important dimension of the work of ministers in Geneva was the weekly meetings ordered by the *Ordinances*. This was to insure purity in the church and agreement on sound doctrine. Disagreements were to be dealt with collectively.

Meetings of the ministers developed into an important feature of the Genevan church, the Company of Pastors (*Compagnie Des Pasteurs*). Ministers gathered at seven o'clock on Friday mornings to participate in Bible study with discussions led by the preachers. These were similar to practices in cities such as Strasbourg and Zurich, where they were called *Kirchenkonvent* and "Prophesyings." Calvin himself always participated fully, providing what amounted to a weekly lecture. He also served as Moderator of the Company. The meetings were public and once a quarter, there was opportunity for "mutual censure," where the doctrine or conduct of a person could be brought up for discussion in the context of Christian concern. This procedure functioned as a way of fostering Christian beliefs being enacted in Christian life.

Genevan ministers were expected to be models of Christian living who avoided sin and dubious practices. The *Ordinances* described differences between "crimes" of ministers and "faults" of ministers. Crimes by ministers—heresy, schism, and rebellion against ecclesiastical order—would be investigated by the assembly of ministers and elders, the results of which would be reported to the magistrate so a guilty person could be deposed. For lesser vices or faults, admonition could be given with ecclesiastical judgment being a "last step."

The ongoing question for Geneva through the years was interpreting and enacting the relations between church and the city government. The magistrates of Geneva saw the Consistory, the combination of pastors and elders, as a cooperative body and instrument of the government. When the Consistory acted, it was doing so as an arm of the local government. In the tensions and struggles that ensued through the years, the church sought to enact its own rights, realizing at well that the civil government was not inclined to give up its powers to any degree. Calvin was involved in the reform of the civil government, seeking to establish a city where the people participated in the government through the various councils, which had defined responsibilities.

CITY GOVERNMENT

Geneva used three Councils to carry out its governmental functions. Each had particular roles to play but they were also interrelated. The Little Council (also Small Council or Senate) was the body charged with the daily running of the city. It had twenty-five members with four administrative leaders called Syndics. The Council of Sixty was composed of the twenty-five members of the Little Council plus thirty-five councilors. Its focus was on diplomatic issues. The thirty-five members of the Little Council who served on the Council of Sixty were drawn from the Council of Two-Hundred. This body approved the legislation proposed by the Little Council. As well, it elected members for the Little Council. All eligible voters of Geneva composed the General Assembly of the city. Male citizens were entitled to vote and hold seats on the three councils. Non-citizens, called "Bourgeois," were those who received this special status by the Small Council. This position could also be bought. Bourgeois could serve on the Council of Sixty, the Council of Two-Hundred, and could vote in the General Assembly. Those who could not vote or hold public office, except for pastor or lecturer, were Habitants. The Little Council could dismiss Habitants from their positions and expel them from the city. Calvin was a Habitant of Geneva until the last five years of his life.[4]

WORSHIP AND CATECHISMS

Central to Geneva church life was worship. The forms of worship laid out by the *Ecclesiastical Ordinances* took a while to be instituted. But attending worship was required in Geneva. Sunday and Wednesday were days when the congregations of the city gathered. The ideal time for the service was an hour. But when the sermon ran longer than expected, the time of the service was lengthened. In switching from traditional Catholicism to the Protestant faith, various elements from the Catholic past continued to have effects in the belief system of Geneva citizens. Only long-term education could help remedy this problem. But most Genevans did attend worship, as well as other gatherings such as the Congrégation or the lectures in theology that Calvin provided.

4. This summary is drawn from Davis, *John Calvin*, 33.

Reports from the 1540s indicate that churches were often overcrowded, a condition made more difficult by the stream of French refugees that flooded the city.

The *Form of Prayers and Ecclesiastical Songs* published in 1542 as well as the *Catechism* gave a reforming structure to worship and to the lives of Genevan Christians. The liturgy prescribed was drawn in large part from the liturgy Calvin used in Strasbourg where Bucer had constructed the worship service. Bucer's prayers were used. The liturgy for Baptism and the Lord's Supper—the church's two sacraments—was composed by Calvin. He borrowed the form for the marriage service from a liturgy by his friend, Farel. Calvin became attached to the church liturgy through the years. Near the time of his death, he recommended to his clergy colleagues that the liturgy not be changed.

In the church building itself, women and men occupied opposite sides of the church. The service proceeded with definite liturgical elements including prayers, readings of the Scriptures, preaching of the sermon, and music. There was no practice of kneeling because that was associated with the earlier Roman Church and was regarded as a superstition relating to the Mass and venerating the elements of the Lord's Supper.

A distinguishing feature of Geneva church worship was the singing of metrical Psalms. This practice developed through the years and was a major way by which Scripture was heard and understood and appropriated by the congregation. When the musician Clément Marot arrived in Geneva, he was employed to produce versifications of the Psalms, on some of which he collaborated with Calvin. Marot left before all the work was completed so that when the Psalm collection appeared in 1545, the Genevan *Psalter*, nine pieces had come from Calvin's own work. The Psalter was important for Calvin who, quoting St. Augustine, indicated that the psalms of David were the very best songs to be sung in worship. The Psalter was a major means of developing the spirituality of the congregation and the individual piety of its members.

Through time, church renovations in Geneva and surrounding parishes reoriented worship spaces. The Roman Mass had emphasized engaging the senses in worship through sight, sound, smell, taste, and touch. The Reformed emphasis was on simplicity in worship in spaces unadorned by any images, which could lead to idolatry. For the Reformed, the ear and mind of the worshiper were to be primarily engaged.

The minds of Genevan worshipers were also engaged by the Catechisms Calvin composed. When he returned to Geneva, Calvin insisted that catechetical instruction be observed, along with the prescriptions of church discipline. The setting for catechetical teaching was Sunday afternoon in the three churches where small children were to assemble. The goal was to acquaint them with the Christian faith in such a way that they would be ready to make a public profession of faith in Jesus Christ. This was the means by which one was admitted to participation in the Lord's Supper. The normal time for this profession of faith to be made was between the child's tenth and fifteenth year, depending on how things went with the catechism classes. A small catechism was prepared by Calvin, in haste he said, to be replaced by his *Instruction et confession de foy* (1537). This catechism summarized his 1536 *Institutes*. It was published in Basel in Latin in 1538 as *Catechismus, sive christianae religionis institution*. The larger catechism Calvin published in 1545 went to a question/answer format and featured 373 questions and answers.[5] Catechisms functioned to indicate

---

5. On the 1537 and 1538 Catechisms, see ch. 2 note 5 above. For the 1545 Catechism see *Calvin: Theological Treatises*, 83–139.

what was being taught in the churches of Geneva. Calvin saw his Latin catechisms as a way of witnessing to the unity of the Christian church. No matter how widespread churches may be, they could be unified in what they believed as pious doctrine, as confessed in the various catechisms the churches produced.

PREACHING, TEACHING, AND LEARNING

In Geneva, Calvin's life took on the contours of daily and weekly routines which he maintained until his death. Chief among his duties was preaching. This he did nearly daily. Eventually, the city provided for stenographers who recorded Calvin's words so his preaching is now preserved. Many sermons are also lost since during the nineteenth-century, a number of them were inadvertently destroyed.

Calvin also lectured on the Scriptures. These lectures formed the basis of the numerous biblical commentaries he published through the years. They also formed the groundwork for the various expansions of his *Institutes of the Christian Religion*, published in Latin and usually followed by a French version from 1536–1560.

Calvin also engaged in numerous theological controversies through the years. He was vigilant to react to views he felt were dangerous to the Geneva church and to the larger body of Protestant churches in general. As Calvin's international reputation grew, he was also consulted by church leaders on various issues. With these and many others, Calvin carried on a voluminous correspondence through the years. Calvin's letters are a source of insight for the varieties of work and issues with which he dealt. Many of these letters serve as a form of pastoral care, Calvin reflecting and advising about particular problems. This was a function Calvin also carried out in Geneva with members of the church. His goal was to find a faithful and theologically responsible way of dealing with what was at hand.

This same motive was also operative in Calvin's work with the various official bodies in the city. He worked with the Consistory as well as the Company of Pastors to try to guide the church into ways of belief, life, and practice that brought glory to God. His struggles with the city council were public expressions of Calvin's convictions about what the will of God was for the here and now.

Calvin's passion for Christian faith informed by the best thought that can be brought to bear fueled his drive to establish a means for educating clergy and those preparing for the ministry. The Genevan Academy was eventually established in 1559 with Calvin's chief assistant, Theodore Beza, as Rector. The Academy had two parts, a Latin school (*schola private*) for youth and the Upper School (*schola publica*) for educating future ministers. The education received in the Academy (which eventually became the University of Geneva) was in service of the church. Students subscribed to the Geneva catechism and the Academy became a source of supplying ministers for Protestant churches throughout Europe. In the last years of his life, Calvin lectured at the Academy three times a week, expounding the Scriptures. So while his participation, overall, was relatively brief, the Academy did serve as part of Calvin's legacy. It marked an institutional counterpart to his *Institutes*, as both instructed clergy and all who were interested in the Christian faith.

5

THE GENEVAN CHURCH (1550–1555)

Calvin's life in Geneva, with all his duties and cares, was not easy. Through the 1540s and later, Calvin faced political battles with authorities as well as theological battles with those who disagreed with his teachings. While in difficult situations, Calvin found strength in biblical figures and verses that spoke of God's aid and grace in times of need. Biblical texts spoke to the realities of his own life in powerful ways.

Not all Genevans approved of Calvin's attempts to reform the church and lives of the citizens. At times, Calvin was physically intimated and threatened. Guns were fired outside the church; and he was ridiculed. As a sign of scorn, some persons named their dogs "Calvin."

An ongoing issue for Calvin was the struggle over the right of excommunication. For Calvin, this was a matter of church discipline and he believed, was a proper duty of the church and its officials in the Consistory. The city council, however, had powers related to the ordering of the church and its life. So tensions were there, and expressed. Calvin was not dismissed from his position through this period, as he and Farel had been in their earliest times in Geneva.

The Genevan Church (1550–1555)

Through it all, the Council did support the reformer and found ways, at points, to work through or avoid more difficult situations.

THE BOLSEC CONTROVERSY

A theological controversy in which Calvin was involved occurred when Jerome (Hieronoymous) Bolsec (d. 1584), a former Carmelite monk who had gone over to the Reformation and became a physician, moved to a city in the vicinity of Geneva in 1550. Bolsec frequently traveled to Geneva to hear Calvin lecture. He was in agreement with Calvin on many points, except on Calvin's views of predestination. Calvin taught that salvation was fully the work of God and that God has eternally chosen who will be saved and who will not be saved. This view is sometimes called "double predestination."

Earlier the two had held a discussion. But on the October 16, 1551 meeting of the weekly Bible study (called the Congrégation) Bolsec publicly criticized the reformer. He accused Calvin of making God the author of sin and urged the assembled people to reject the false teachings of their ministers. Calvin had argued that Bolsec reversed the proper order of God's work: election, whereby God determines salvation, comes before faith, which is the means by which salvation or election is realized. By making faith come first, Calvin said Bolsec was putting faith and salvation within human control. God's election was dependent on what people do. This, Calvin believed, was unbiblical.

Because Bolsec had attacked the preaching and teachings of the established church, he was charged with heresy by the civil authorities. Wrong viewpoints that endangered the eternal salvation of their hearers were serious matters and must be dealt with, was the thinking. After consulting with churches at Basel, Berne, and Zurich, which did not come forth as strongly as Calvin would have liked, the magistrates found there were grounds for heresy. If they had supported Bolsec, they would have been rejecting the teachings of Calvin whom the city employed to preach and teach the Bible. That would have amounted to the Council rejecting itself.

On December 18, Calvin made a presentation on the doctrine of election or predestination. The Geneva ministers endorsed Calvin's views, which were eventually published in 1562. Bolsec received his sentence from the civil authorities. He was banished from Geneva for life. He moved to Berne, where, on Calvin's insistence, the city took measures against him. So he fled to Paris and returned to the Roman Catholic Church. In 1577, Bolsec published a biography of Calvin, based on lies and slander, which presented the picture of Calvin as a villain and tyrant of the city of Geneva.

THE CASE OF MICHAEL SERVETUS

The most famous incident of Calvin's ministry in Geneva was the case of Michael Servetus. Calvin's role in this case brought him praise from Christians in other nations during Calvin's time. Since, it has become a symbol of what some regard as Calvin's evil and bloodthirsty nature and the kinds of results to which his theology leads. When the case is viewed as a disagreement over two opinions, it seems Servetus's execution was an unmitigated act of violence enacted by a tyrant. But Calvin's actions were what would have been expected in his sixteenth-century context in the face of theological beliefs the church found dangerous. But more, when civil governments put people to death for religious heresies, they were acting in the main to preserve

The Genevan Church (1550–1555)

civil order. In contrast to executions for heresy that were a common part of European life, the death of Servetus was the sole instance of an execution for religious beliefs that occurred in Geneva during Calvin's lifetime.

Servetus, born about the same time as Calvin, was a "Renaissance man." He was a scholar in several fields whose studies in human anatomy anticipated the later work of William Harvey who published theories about the circulation of the blood in 1628. Theologically, Servetus used the humanist motto, "Back to the Sources" to try to set Christianity on a new footing. His *Christianismi restitutio* (1553), published anonymously, disputed many Christian doctrines, including the Trinity, original sin, infant baptism, and justification by faith among others. Servetus tried to show that his views about God and Christ were consistent with the beliefs of the earliest Christians. In Servetus's view, Roman Catholicism as well as Reformation churches had destroyed contemporary Christianity.

Servetus's view of God was that instead of a Holy Trinity, taught by orthodox Christianity, God was known through many names, each meant to convey a particular message about God. The names of "Jesus" and "Holy Spirit" were just two of these names. In correspondence carried on with Calvin before he showed up in Geneva on August 1553, Servetus referred to the Trinity as a "three-headed Cerberus," referring to the Greek and Roman mythological figure, which was a multiheaded dog or "hellhound," with a serpent's tail, a mane of snakes, and lion's claws. The hound guarded the entrance of the underworld in order to keep the dead from escaping the underworld and the living from entering it.

Servetus, under assumed names, was known throughout Europe as possessing heretical views. When he appeared in Geneva at a worship service on August 13, 1553, he was recognized and Calvin was informed. He reported this to the magistrates who imprisoned Servetus through a complaint that contained thirty-nine particulars filed by Calvin's secretary, Nicholas de la Fontaine. Nicholas, acting on behalf of Calvin, who was the accuser, was imprisoned with Servetus until the beginning of the trial, under the law of the time.

When proceedings began, Geneva consulted other cities on what direction to take. The cities agreed Servetus's teachings should be condemned because he had departed from the Word of God. But they did not prescribe to Geneva what particular punishment to enact.

During the trial, Calvin served as an expert theological witness, as he had during the Bolsec case. On October 26, 1553, the magistrates of the Council reached their verdict. It was the civil authority that made the decision on Servetus's fate, not Calvin. The decision was death by being burned at the stake. The decision was based primarily on Servetus's denial of the Trinity, which was considered a key part of Christian belief. Those who denied the Trinity were considered enemies of the state and dangers to a society which sought to preserve Christian truth. Servetus's view that those who believed in the Trinity were atheists put him outside the acceptable limits of church and society.

Calvin asked that Servetus be beheaded instead of burnt at the stake. But his request was denied. Calvin and Farel both visited Servetus in prison on October 27, the day of his execution. Servetus pled for mercy, which was not in Calvin's power to grant. After again trying to convince Servetus of the truth of the Trinity, no change was made. As he was brought to the stake, Servetus cried: "Jesus, Son of the eternal God, take pity on me." This statement did not attribute divinity to Jesus ("Son of the eternal God"), which

The Genevan Church (1550–1555)

would have been the case had Servetus been able to affirm Jesus as "the eternal Son of God."

The Geneva Council's decision on Servetus gained praise from nearly all principal Protestant leaders. Urged to justify the decision and Geneva's approach, Calvin published his *Defense of the Orthodox Faith of the Doctrine of the Trinity* (1554). This work, endorsed by Geneva's clergy, defended the church's historic, orthodox teachings on the Trinity, especially in light of the errors of Servetus. It also defended the actions of magistrates against heretical teachings. Throughout Europe, Calvin's reputation as a defender of the faith grew in light of the Servetus case.

GAINING SUPPORT

Throughout his time in Geneva, Calvin had faced opposition in various forms. The waves of immigrants that streamed into Geneva, especially from France, brought a spate of anti-French feeling, some of it directed at "that Frenchman," Calvin, whom opponents believed wanted to gain power in the city and to rule like Roman Catholic bishops had done in the past.

Things became focused in 1555. The leader of those who opposed Calvin and whom he called "Libertines," Ami Perrin and his "Perrinists," were accused of treason and disgraced. This led to a landslide defeat of the anti-Calvin party in the February 1555 elections. When a large number of French refugees were given citizenship in the spring, those who objected threatened to take power back. But nothing materialized after some leaders were arrested and others left the city. This meant the majority of the Council was now behind Calvin. Now he could hope to enact more fully the rule of Christ and his Word in the city of Geneva.

6

FINAL YEARS (1556-1564)

THE FINAL YEARS OF Calvin's ministry in Geneva were spent in consolidating and continuing to work at the reform of the church, which was his ongoing passion. At the same time, he became more engaged in issues outside Geneva.

The status of ecclesiastical discipline was boosted in November 1557 when the Geneva Council passed a law prescribing contempt for the *Ecclesiastical Ordinances* was considered as rebellion. The penalty was banishment from the city for a year. In 1560, Calvin and Viret argued for a stronger separation of ecclesiastical work from the civil functions of the magistracy. This led to four provisions that set the church's ecclesiastical work as separate from the city government. On November 13, 1561, these changes were announced and revised articles were set. Every three years, people would be required to swear allegiance to them in church.

Calvin also assisted in adjusting some of the civil laws, his lawyerly training again coming in handy. Legislation about morality strongly promoted marriage as the good norm while strongly punishing prostitution and fornication. Luxurious clothing and meals were restricted and

Final Years (1556–1564)

sobriety was to be the note, even on festive occasions. At the same time, the city government helped established a weaving mill and was able to compete with businesses in France.

Calvin's passion for his homeland was reinforced by his desires to train pastors who could reenter France and reclaim the land for the Protestant faith. The Geneva Academy, which opened on June 5, 1559, became a leading center for educating future pastors whose ministries extended across Europe. This international outreach helped spread the Reformed faith and enhanced Geneva's stature as a "mother church" for Reformed churches.

Calvin's vision for the city and beyond was of a place where true doctrine was preached and heard and lived. Changes in Geneva from the Roman Catholicism of earlier times to a reforming Protestantism were the evolving events. But more was needed. People themselves must imbibe the true faith and have their whole lives oriented to a single purpose: living in faith and obedience to God, seeking God's glory not their own. This kind of radical transformation could come only through the continuing presentation of God's Word in Scripture, by teaching and preaching and its appropriation in the lives of hearers by the power of the Holy Spirit. Everyone in society, no matter what their social class, must live in this way for the church to be faithful to its Lord and Master, Jesus Christ. God's will for the church body, for society, and for all Christian believers is for all to live faithfully, focused on the gospel of Jesus Christ. A glimmer of that vision in Geneva was caught in the famous statement of the Scots Reformer John Knox (1514–1572) who studied in Geneva and went on to be a leader of the Scottish Reformation. Knox said: "I can affirm without hesitation that in this place that in this place is found the most perfect school of Christ that ever was in the earth since the days of the apostles. In other places I confess Christ be truly preached; but manners and religion to be so seriously reformed, I have not yet seen in any other place besides."[1]

CALVIN'S FINAL DAYS AND DEATH

John Calvin had never been in good health. During his years in Geneva, his health worsened as he struggled in pain against a number of ailments. These included gout, kidney stones, chronic pulmonary tuberculosis, pleurisy, rheumatism, and migraine headaches.[2]

During the winter 1558–59, Calvin was very ill. His brother, Antoine helped him prepare the 1559 edition of his *Institutes* and the following year, a French edition appeared. When the Geneva Academy opened in June 1559, he was better and continued his activities. But by 1564, he had to give up much of his work due to his poor health.

Calvin gave his last lecture on February 2, 1564, on a portion of the book of Ezekiel. His last sermon was preached on February 6. He traveled to the city hall for the final time on March 27 and attended his last meeting of the Consistory the next day. On Easter Sunday, April 2, in church Calvin participated in the Lord's Supper for the last time.

On April 25, Calvin dictated his will. He was thankful for God's grace and indicated he had done the most he could with the grace given to him for preaching and interpreting the Scriptures purely and faithfully.

Calvin's farewell words to members of the Small Council were given on April 27 at his home, because he was

1. In van t'Spijker, *Calvin*, 108.
2. Cited in Davis, *John Calvin*, 51, from Cooke, "Calvin's Illnesses and Their Relation to Christian Vocation," 41–52. I was present for Dr. Cooke's lecture. It was graphically, visually illustrated!

Final Years (1556–1564)

too weak to leave his house. The next day he commended the ministers to the care of Beza. Calvin wanted to communicate to these colleagues his commitment to the work God had given while also indicating his weaknesses along the way. From his bed, Calvin said:

> I have had many infirmities which you have been obliged to bear with, and what is more, all I have done has been worth nothing. The ungodly will greedily seize upon this word, but I say it again that all I have done has been worth nothing, and that I am a miserable creature. But certainly I can say this, that I have willed what is good, that my vices have always displeased me, and that the root of the fear of God has been in my heart; and you may say that the disposition was good, and I pray you, that the evil be forgiven me.[3]

Calvin the human person possessed a short temper. He could be impatient and could give the appearance of being arrogant and prideful. Calvin confessed once to Bucer "Alas, it is true that with none of my great and numerous shortcomings have I wrestled harder than with such impatience. Yes, I am making some progress, but I have never reached the point yet of keeping this wild beast completely under control."[4]

As he waited for death, Calvin was fully lucid and received friends who visited. His old colleague, Farel, was able to visit after receiving Calvin's parting note of May 2. On May 19, the ministers held their weekly meeting at Calvin's house. On May 27, John Calvin died. He was buried the next day in an unmarked grave, according to his request.

---

3. In van't Spijker, *Calvin*, 123.
4. In ibid., 124.

PART TWO
THEOLOGY OF CALVIN

CALVIN'S THEOLOGY DEVELOPED OVER time and is found in his numerous writings. The traditional place to look for Calvin's theological insights is his *Institutes of the Christian Religion*. As we have seen, the *Institutes* developed from the earliest 1536 edition through new editions in Latin and French to the final Latin edition of 1559 and then the French edition of 1560. The 1559 *Institutes* has been the main way into Calvin's theology since it is highly structured, developed, and deals with theological topics.

Today, Calvin scholars emphasize Calvin's work as a biblical interpreter as a key source for Calvin's insights as well. The *Institutes* was Calvin's theological statement, based on his continuing work of interpreting the Bible in his lectures, commentaries, and sermons. The *Institutes* "gathers up" Calvin's biblical insights into a more systematic statement. But it is also important to recognize that a purpose of this theological work, the *Institutes*, was to help persons understand the overall message of the Bible itself. The *Institutes* provides a framework for understanding Scripture. So the convictions Calvin came to in the process of interpreting the Bible in lecturing, writings, and sermons are important elements of his overall theology.

In our survey of Calvin's theology, we will look primarily to the *Institutes* as the most developed expression of Calvin's thought. The hope is that this survey of the *Institutes* will lead to further explorations of Calvin's other writings, including his commentaries and sermons. All these together convey the lifeblood of what Calvin believed and taught. All the sources are important.

The clearest way to pursue Calvin's thought is to follow the flow of the *Institutes*. We will use the 1559 *Institutes* as our roadmap for an overview of what Calvin considered most important. Not every topic with which Calvin deals will be covered. But we will look at the key elements of his overall theological understanding.

The *Institutes* is divided into four "books." These are:

1. One: The Knowledge of God the Creator

2. The Knowledge of God the Redeemer in Christ, First Disclosed to the Fathers Under the Law, and Then to Us in the Gospel

3. The Way in Which We Receive the Grace of Christ: What Benefits Come to Us from It, and What Effects Follow

4. The External Means or Aids by Which God Invites Us into the Society of Christ and Holds Us Therein

These topics and arrangement emerged over the years as the *Institutes* went through revisions. Scholars disagree on what Calvin contended to convey by the arrangement. Some see Calvin as following the traditional order of the Apostles' Creed with a sequence of considering God the Father, Jesus Christ the Son, the Holy Spirit, and the church. Or, when we look at the titles of the first two books, we see they are The Knowledge of God the Creator, and The Knowledge of God the Redeemer. These are the two major divisions of how God is known—as the Father in Creation, and as the Son in Redemption, or Salvation. Another suggestion has been that Calvin is concerned throughout the *Institutes* with the interplay of the knowledge of God and the knowledge of ourselves, a relationship he discusses at the beginning of the *Institutes*.

7

BOOK I

The Knowledge of God the Creator

CLEARLY, "KNOWLEDGE" IS AN important category for Calvin. "Knowledge" for him does not primarily refer to "intellectual knowledge" obtained by human reason, the kind of knowledge we deal with in our everyday lives. Instead, "knowledge of God" is what is important. It is our knowledge of who God is and what God does. For Calvin, the Scriptures are this source of knowledge. It is knowledge that has an intellectual dimension to it because it is something that can be stated and understood. But the knowledge of God the Scriptures convey is primarily experiential knowledge or relational knowledge. It is "heart knowledge" as well as "head knowledge." It is the knowledge of God we experience as we deal with the living God. This God is known to us in creation and in the salvation God has given in Jesus Christ. This knowledge is crucial for life because it deals with the most important questions we face: Who is God? and What has God Done? Even more, this question presses us to the issue of how we stand in relation to this knowledge of God. Do we *know* the God of whom the Scriptures speak in a personal and experiential way? Or, do we treat the knowledge of God as only an intellectual curiosity or one thing among the many things we know about or may think about?

So "knowledge of God" was important for Calvin in very real ways. Through the *Institutes* he explores who God is and what God is done. He explores how humans are aware of God; what relationship they have to God; and what God has done in Jesus Christ, to change and transform human beings. These great questions are ones Calvin probes. They are ones important for his times as well as for our own; and for each of us.

KNOWING GOD AND KNOWING OURSELVES (1.1–2)

Calvin begins with the famous statement that endured through numerous editions of the *Institutes*: "Nearly all the wisdom we possess, that is to say, true and sound wisdom, consists of two parts: the knowledge of God and of ourselves" (1.1.1). This links these two objects of knowledge—which are the most important knowledges with which we have to deal.

There is a relationship between these. Calvin says that without the knowledge of ourselves, we cannot have a knowledge of God. Without a knowledge of God, we can have no knowledge of ourselves. But which comes first? This is a quandry, a "chicken and egg" question. We can't really know which comes first. They are actually inseparable from each other. "Who is God?" "Who Am I?" These are the big questions.

When we ask, "Who Am I?" we can think of ourselves in certain ways. But we are naturally led to ask: Where did I come from? What is the purpose of my life? How shall I live? When we pose these questions, we are drawn to think of "God," our creator (Acts 17:28). We can't really know who we are, unless we have "looked upon God's face" (sec. 2).

When we ask, "Who is God?" we can think of many things. But we wonder how does this "God" relate to me? Is God just "neutral energy" somewhere "up there"? What is the nature of this God? Is God personal? Is God knowable? The questions throng.

Calvin recognizes these questions are inseparable. While he says we can't decide which comes first, he proposes that a good order of teaching is to consider first the knowledge of God and then the knowledge of ourselves (sec. 3).

For Calvin, the purpose of the knowledge of God is not an intellectual purpose, or to enable us only to "conceive that there is a God." What we really need is to know God in a personal way. Calvin said we cannot say, "properly speaking," that "God is known where there is no religion or piety" (1.2.1). This puts the knowledge of God into the personal realm. We may say that God is the creator, or that people should honor and adore God. But we need also to be "persuaded that he is the fountain of every good, and that we must seek nothing elsewhere than in him." God may sustain the universe and rule humanity by God's righteousness and judgment; but we also need to know of God's mercy that watches over us.

Then Calvin gives what is a classic definition of piety, a word we don't use too much, except perhaps often in a negative sense, that someone is making a "show" of their piety, for instance. But for Calvin, piety is basic because it defines the relationship between God the creator and all of us as creatures. Calvin said, "I call 'piety' that reverence joined with love of God which the knowledge of his benefits induces" (1.2.1). We not only "reverence" God our creator; we love this God. We have a personal relationship with God. We love God—because we know who God is and what God has done—God's benefits to us, induce our love. So "piety" defines the relationship between us and God. God has given benefits to us, which as we will see come especially in Jesus Christ; and which come purely from God's love for us, undeserved as it is. This is God's "grace." We respond to God's gracious benefits by reverencing God and by loving God.

So the knowledge of God involves trust and reverence. What purpose would there be to "know" a God with whom we have nothing to do (sec.2)? Instead, our knowledge should teach us fear and reverence for God, then guide us to seek every good from God, and give God the credit when all good is received. We acknowledge God to be "the fountainhead and source of every good." This leads us to cleave to God and trust God. Only the depravity of humans, their sin, turns us away from this kind of relationship. The truly pious person will recognize that God governs all things, trusting God to be a guide through life, protecting us as we trust in God. Indeed, since God is good and merciful, we can live with "perfect trust" and not doubt God's "help." For in God's "loving-kindness a remedy will be provided" for our ills. The pious person will observe God's authority in all things, reverence God's majesty, and take care to advance God's glory and obey God's commandments. Indeed, even if there were no "hell" or punishment, the pious person would shudder at offending God.

THE KNOWLEDGE OF GOD IN US (1.3–5)

Where does knowledge of God come from? Calvin believes that, within humans, there is an "awareness of divinity" (Lat. *Divinitatis sensus*) naturally implanted in us. We have a sense of deity within our hearts. This sense of divinity, engraved in our minds can never be erased. So actual "godliness" is impossible (1.3; cf. Romans 1:18–32)!

But there is a problem. Humans suppress this sense of there being a God; they turn away from it; they fashion a "god" in their own image and consciously turn away from the true God (1.4). Instead of loving God their creator, humans sin by rebelling and stifling the knowledge of God. Even all around us, there are the evidences of God. Look at nature. Calvin said we cannot open our eyes without being compelled to see God. For "wherever you cast your eyes, there is no spot in the universe wherein you cannot discern at least some sparks" of God's glory (1.5.1). The divine wisdom is on display for all to see (sec. 2). Human beings themselves are an example of God's goodness and wisdom, a "mirror of God's works" (sec. 3).

But the problem persists. Humans turn ungratefully against their creator. Instead of praising God, their pride prevents them, so signs of divinity are concealed and suppressed. They confuse the creature with the creator, basically constructing "a shadow deity to drive away the true God, whom we should fear and adore" (1.5.5). God is the Lord of creation and the one to whom faith and worship should be directed. Natural phenomena around us witness to God's power while in God's providence goodness comes to us (1.6–7). But people, immersed in their own errors, are "struck blind in such a dazzling theater" (1.5.8). Though the heavens and earth are a theater of God's glory and majesty, humans are not true spectators of it.

Though nature is a visible image of the invisible God, we need a true knowledge of God that is not speculative, which "merely flits in the brain," but a knowledge of God the creator that "takes root in the heart" (1.5.9). We need to know God from the works God does. This knowledge would arouse us to worship and encourage us to hope for eternal life (1.5.10).

So the story of humanity living before its creator is that the evidence of God's creation does not bring us knowledge of God. Humans fail to know and worship God, falling into superstition and confusion (1.5.11–12). The human mind is like a "labyrinth," full of frustration and confusion while humans fashion idols in place of God. So evidences of God do not speak to us; they cannot lead us to a knowledge of God (1.15.14; Rom. 1:19). The fault in all this is within us, says Calvin. We have no excuse because we cannot claim ignorance (1.5.15). Humans "corrupt the seed" of the knowledge of God, not giving glory to God the creator. So theologically, humans are inexcusable before God.

ANOTHER AND BETTER HELP: THE SCRIPTURES (1.6–9)

Humans need help, which God has provided. Calvin's discussion of the Holy Scriptures describes the Bible as "another and better help" to "direct us aright to the very Creator of the universe" (1.6.1). God adds the light of God's Word to enable us to know God unto salvation.

Calvin uses the image of "spectacles" to indicate how the Scriptures provide the knowledge of God we need to receive:

> Just as old or bleary-eyed men and those with weak vision, if you thrust before them a most beautiful volume, even if they recognize it to be some sort of writing, yet can scarcely construe two words, but with the aid of spectacles will begin to read distinctly; so Scripture, gathering up the otherwise confused knowledge of God in our minds, having dispersed our dullness, clearly shows us the true God. (1.6.1)

God opens God's "most hallowed lips" to put before us God's "Word," a "more direct and more certain mark whereby he is to be recognized."

The Scriptures present us with the knowledge of God the Creator (being discussed in book I of the *Institutes*) as well as the knowledge of God the Redeemer (in book II). For Calvin, Scripture provides the account of God's speaking to patriarchs of old and to prophets who interpreted God's law. Without these accounts in Scripture, we would fall into error (1.6.2, 3). For Scripture can communicate to us what God's revelation in God's works cannot (1.6.4).

The Scriptures are "the Word of God" and gain their authority when they are recognized as "having sprung from heaven, as if there the living words of God were heard" (1.7.1). It is a "pernicious error," said Calvin, to think that Scripture gains its authority only by the consent of the church—the view of the Roman Catholic Church. Instead, the church itself is grounded in the teachings of the prophets and the apostles (1.7.2; cf. Eph. 2:20).

It is the Holy Spirit who witnesses to Scripture's authority and this witness is the highest proof that Scripture comes from God. The Spirit's testimony within us is stronger than human reasons, judgments, or conjectures. It is the Spirit's work that convinces us that Scripture comes from God and is "God's Sacred Word" (1.7.4). This testimony of the Spirit is "more excellent than all reason." God is the best witness to God's Word and Scripture will not find acceptance in the human heart "before it is sealed by the inward testimony of the Spirit." By the work of the Spirit, the Scripture is "self-authenticated" and we gain certainty that the Scripture is God's Word (1.7.5). For Calvin, like Luther, God's Word and God's Spirit are bound up together. The Spirit convinces us that "Scripture is from God" and has "come to us through the ministry of human writers." This is what each believer, or the "elect," experience in recognizing the Scriptures as God's Word, the place where they "hearken to God's voice."

While Calvin says there are proofs at hand from human reason to establish the credibility of Scripture, these only gain credibility with us once we have accepted the Scriptures by the witness of the Holy Spirit (1.8). Some of these proofs are the antiquity of Scripture, miracles, prophesies, and the blood of the martyrs. But none of these, or all of these, cannot replace the witness of the Spirit to Scripture's authority. A saving knowledge of God comes only when our certainty about Scripture is founded in the inner witness or persuasion of the Holy Spirit (1.8.4).

Calvin rejects those who appeal only to the Holy Spirit within themselves as the source for revelation, claiming to be inspired by the Spirit without regard to the Scripture. These are "rascals" (1.9.1) who are treating God's Word with contempt. Instead, the Holy Spirit does not concoct "new and unheard of revelations" to lead us away from received doctrines. Rather the Spirit seals our minds with the doctrine the gospel commends.

What is key for Calvin is that Word and Spirit are inextricably bound up together (1.9.2–3). There is a mutual bond between the Spirit who confirms the Word within us and the Word that comes alive through the illumination of God's Spirit for believers. When we separate that which God has joined together, trouble appears. This means that God's Word in Scripture has no effect unless its readers are illumined by God's Spirit. God's Spirit will never lead us in ways that are incongruent or contrary to God's Word. This prescription of holding Word and Spirit together continues to be a key insight for the church today, as well as for those who read and interpret Scripture in a Christian context.

GOD THE CREATOR (1.10–12)

While the knowledge of God is set forth in the created universe, it is "more vividly revealed" in God's Word (1.10). The purpose of this knowledge of God is to invite us to fear God, trust in God, and to worship God as we depend on God's goodness.

Calvin was adamant, as he believed Scripture was, that no visible form of God should be made (1.11). No pictorial representations or images should be fashioned with human hands. This is idolatry, specifically forbidden in the Ten Commandments (Exodus 20:4). True religion binds us to the one and only God (1.12).

The one, true God who is known to us in the Scriptures is a God who is infinite and spiritual. The Bible presents God in ways that are understandable to us as humans—as having a mouth, ears, eyes, hands, and feet. But this is God's style of communication, according to Calvin. He refers to the idea of "accommodation," a key concept throughout his theology. It has its roots in the ancient rhetoricians of Rome who realized that in order to communicate with an audience, their message must be presented in a way that is understandable to its audience. So the rhetoricians "adjusted" their speech to the capacities of their audiences. What they said must be understandable to their listeners. This seems like common sense to us. We know that we will talk in a different way to children than we do to adults. We "accommodate" our communication to the capacities of our hearers. So, Calvin wrote against those who argued that God was "corporeal"—had a body—because the Scriptures mention God's "mouth," "hands," etc. He said, "For who even of slight intelligence does not understand that, as nurses commonly do with infants, God is wont in a measure to 'lisp' in speaking to us? Thus such forms of speaking do not so much express clearly what God is like as accommodate the knowledge of him to our slight capacity. To do this he must descend far beneath his loftiness." (1.13.1). Scripture is God's way of communicating with humans. Accommodation is God's way of bridging the gap between God and humanity. God communicated God's divine message through human writers. Instead of requiring humans to learn "God language" to communicate with God, God learned human languages—God used everyday, human writers to present God's Word in human words. Scripture is God's divine message communicated through human writers. Scripture is an example of God's way of reaching out to humans in ways we can understand.[1]

TRINITY (1.13)

The true God presented in Scripture is distinguished from idols. The true God is one God in three persons. Calvin relies on the historic church's use of Greek terms to make the distinctions necessary to understand scriptural teachings. While the term "Trinity" does not appear in the Bible itself, Calvin believed the terms associated with it are appropriate interpretations of Scripture and are therefore legitimate to use to help us understand Scripture (1.13.3).

The church has seen it necessary to use terms such as "Trinity" and "Person" to protect its teachings from false doctrine (1.13.4). For example, in the early church, Arius said Christ was the Son of God. But he also said Christ was created; and had a beginning. The church decided the Greek term, *homoousios*, meaning "of the same substance (essence)," was what it believed about who Jesus Christ is. Arius could not subscribe to this term. He believed Christ

---

1. See Battles, "God Was Accommodating Himself to Human Capacity," 21–42.

was of a "similar substance (essence)" (Gr. *homoiousios*). But "similar" is not "same." So for Arius, Christ was a creature, the first creature God created, instead of being "of the same substance" as God. The early church rejected Arius' teachings. The orthodox view of the Trinity was that the one God, is eternally three Persons: Father, Son, and Holy Spirit (1.13.6).

Calvin discusses both the Deity (divinity) of the Son, Jesus Christ (1.13.7–13), and the Deity (divinity) of the Holy Spirit (1.13.14–15). Jesus Christ is the "Word of God," the eternal Son of God. The Word was "from the beginning with God, was at the same time the cause of all things, together with God the Father [John 1:1–3]" (1.13.7). "Unchangeable," said Calvin, "the Word abides everlastingly one and the same with God, and is God himself."

The Holy Spirit is also God. It is the Spirit who, "everywhere diffused, sustains all things, causes them to grow, and quickens them in heaven and earth" (1.13.14), among other activities.

God is Trinity (triune)—Oneness" (1.13.16) and "Threeness" (1.13.17). The three persons are one, yet three—something no human analogies can capture for us. The Scriptures makes distinctions among the Persons: the Father is the beginning of activity; the fountain and wellspring of all things; the Son is wisdom, counsel (plan) and the ordered disposition of all things; the Spirit is the power and efficacy of that activity (1.13.18).

In each of the three Persons, the fullness and whole nature of the Godhead resides, even as each has distinctive characteristics (1.13.19). The three are interrelated to each other, sharing the same divine essence or nature. The names "Father," "Son" and "Holy Spirit" imply this relationship. In short, "the whole essence of God is spiritual, in which are comprehended Father, Son, and Spirit" (1.13.20). For

Calvin, the Scriptures point us to what the church confesses as the triune God: One God in Three Persons. This view is to be maintained against all heresies (1.13.21–29).

ANGELS AND DEMONS (1.14.1–19)

Calvin viewed angels as celestial beings, created by God, whose ministry and service God uses to carry out God's purposes on earth (1.13.3–12). They act as protectors and helpers of believers (sec. 6), though Calvin did not believe in specific "guardian angels" assigned to specific persons. Instead, "all the heavenly host" look out for each of us. Angels should not be worshiped since divine glory belongs not to them, but to God (1.13.10–12).

Demons are God's adversaries, led by "Satan" or the "Devil" who set themselves against God's kingdom of righteousness (1.13.13–19). This is an irreconcilable struggle of God against the consummate depravity of the devil (sec. 15). The devil and others revolted against God and fell into degeneration and ruin, becoming also the instruments of others as they wage war against the kingdom of God (sec. 16).

Yet the devil and the powers of evil stand under the power of God. Calvin vehemently denies that "believers can ever be conquered or overwhelmed" by these evil powers (sec. 18). Ultimately, "Christ, by dying, conquered Satan" so victory is assured to the children of God.

CREATOR AND CREATION (1.14.20–22)

Despite evil powers at work in the world, believers can "take pious delight in the works of God" in what Calvin refers to as "this most beautiful theater"—the created order all around us which we see "wherever we cast our eyes"

(1.14.20–22; sec. 20). There is a greatness and abundance of creation.

God is the Creator. God, "by the power of his Word and Spirit created heaven and earth out of nothing" and brought forth all living beings as well as inanimate things of every kind (sec. 20). God continues to nourish what God created, renewing them by the gift of propagation in this spacious and abundant house of nature. God especially created humans, as the "most excellent example" of God's works and adorned them with "goodly beauty, and with such great and numerous gifts."

All the attributes of God shine forth in creation (cf. 1.5.1–4), as "all creatures, as in mirrors" show the "immense riches" of God's wisdom, justice, goodness, and power on which we should recollect repeatedly (sec. 21). How should we view God's works? What does it mean for us that God is Creator of heaven and earth?

Calvin says we should not "pass over in ungrateful thoughtlessness or forgetfulness" those powers God shows forth. Rather we should learn to apply those powers to ourselves so that our very hearts are touched. This kind of contemplation of God's goodness in the creation will lead us to thankfulness and trust. For "God has destined all things for our good and salvation." We can feel God's power and grace within ourselves and in the "great benefits" God has given us. This bestirs us to trust, invoking God, praise, and love of God (sec. 22). God has created all things for the sake of humanity and prepared what is useful for us, including the salvation we most need. This leads us not to ingratitude, but to acknowledging every benefit we receive as a blessing from God, to await the fullness of all good things from God alone and "to trust completely that he will never leave us destitute of what we need for salvation"—in short, "to hang our hopes on none but him!" "So," said Calvin, "invited by the great sweetness of his beneficence and goodness, let us study to love and serve him with all our heart." This is what the good Creator and the good creation mean for humans.

HUMAN NATURE (1.15)

Humans were created by God, according to Genesis 1, and are the "noblest and most remarkable example" of God's justice, wisdom, and goodness. We need to know who humans were created to be by their Creator, if we are to have a clear knowledge of God—as Calvin began his *Institutes* by saying (1.1.1). We need to know what we humans were like when we were first created; and what our condition has become after the fall of Adam (Genesis 3). For Calvin, humans were created with an "originally upright nature" (sec. 1; cf. 1.15.1).

Calvin has what is called a "dichotomous" view of humans. That is, humans are "body" and "soul"(sec. 2).[2] The soul is the "nobler part" of humans, which is immortal, yet created essence. For Calvin, the term "spirit" means the same as "soul," except when the two terms are used together. As in Greek philosophy, Calvin referred to the soul as related to the "prison house of the body." The soul is liberated from the body at death.

The "soul" is the "proper seat" of what is the most important factor about humans as created by God. Humans are created in the image of God (Lat. *imago Dei*; Genesis 1:26–28). This separates humans from animals and the rest of creation. In some way, humans are formed in the image and likeness of God, a theological reality which gives a

---

2. See McKim, *The Westminster Dictionary of Theological Terms*, 2nd ed., s.v. "Dichotomism."

spiritual dimension to who humans are created to be. There is a relationship with God the Creator, implied in these terms.

Calvin does not see a difference between "image" and "likeness" as terms (sec. 3; see Genesis 1:26). They reflect Hebrew parallelism in which a second term is regarded as having the same meaning as the first, or, expressing one thing twice. For Calvin, God created humans in whom God would "represent himself as in an image, by means of engraved marks of likeness." The first human, Adam, was created with the integrity of that image and likeness of God, which he knew and which he enjoyed when he kept to "right understanding" and kept his affections "within the bounds of reason, all his senses tempered in right order." While the "primary seat" of the divine image was in the mind and heart, or in the soul and its powers, there was "no part" of humans, "not even the body itself, in which some sparks did not glow." We know most clearly what it means for humans to be created in the image of God when we look at what it means for sinful humans—humans affected by the power of sin which sets them at enmity with God—to be restored to the image of God through Jesus Christ.

The fall of Adam into sin (Genesis 3) affected the relationship of love and trust that God intended to have with humanity. This fall did not mean, says Calvin, that God's image was "totally annihilated and destroyed in him, yet it was so corrupted that whatever remains is frightful deformity" (sec. 4). What is needed for the "recovery of salvation" is the "restoration which we obtain through Christ, who also is called the Second Adam for the reason that he restores us to true and complete integrity" (cf. 1 Cor 15:45). The purpose of the regeneration or "new life" which Jesus Christ brings to the world is "that Christ should reform us to God's image" (cf. Col 3:10; Eph 4:24).

This renewal of the image of God in Christ brings knowledge, as well as pure righteousness and holiness. Because Christ himself is "the most perfect image of God," if we are, says Calvin, "conformed to it, we are so restored that with true piety, righteousness, purity, and intelligence we bear God's image."

This restoration or "salvation" is needed given the effects of sin on created humans. Calvin explained, when he wrote:

> Now God's image is the perfect excellence of human nature which shone in Adam before his defection, but was subsequently so vitiated and almost blotted out that nothing remains after the ruin except what is confused, mutilated, and disease-ridden. Therefore in some part it now is manifest in the elect, in so far as they have been reborn in the spirit; but it will attain its full splendor in heaven. (sec. 4)

This is as grim as possible a portrait of the result of human sin. The only human hope is restoration of the image of God in Jesus Christ by "the grace and power of the Spirit" (sec. 5).

How did humans get this way?

Calvin believed God provided the first human, "Adam," with a soul that had a mind that enabled him to distinguish good from evil, right from wrong, and "what should be followed from what should be avoided" (sec. 8). To this was joined the will, which controlled human choice. As created by God, the human will was "completely amenable to the guidance of the reason." This meant that "man by free will had the power, if he so willed, to attain eternal life." So, "Adam could have stood if he wished, seeing that he fell solely by his own will. But it was because his will was capable of being bent to one side or the other, and was not given the constancy to persevere, that he fell so easily." This meant that, in the story, Adam's will was "in neutral," freely able to choose to sin and disobey God, or not to sin and to obey God.

But Adam chose to sin and in the story in Genesis 3, he and Eve were banished from the Garden of Eden. At this point, Calvin wrote that "man" (humanity) was "far different at the first creation from his whole posterity, who, deriving their origin from him in his corrupted state, have contracted from him a hereditary taint." The free choice to sin and disobey rested with Adam. This made Adam "inexcusable." For posterity, the "choice" is not the same. More will be said of that, later (see 2.1–2).

PROVIDENCE (1.16–18)

The God who created the world is also the God who sustains the world. Calvin maintains that we see as much divine power in the continuing of the universe as there is in its creation or inception. This continuing power of God as governor and preserver of the world is called God's providence.

God's creation and providence are inseparably joined. Anyone might look around and conclude there is a God who created the universe. But truly to grasp what "God is Creator" means is to go on by faith to penetrate more deeply. This leads to the recognition that God keeps the "celestial frame" intact but also that God "sustains, nourishes, and cares for, everything he has made, even to the least sparrow [cf. Matt. 10:29]" (1.16. 1, 2).

God's involvement with the world is so total that there is no such thing as fortune or chance (sec. 2). For all things happen in accord with God's will. God "so regulates all things that nothing takes place without his deliberation," says Calvin (sec. 3). God governs all, not just by a universal law of nature, but by the direct action of God in the events of the world and human life. This brings believers to praise God's omnipotence since God is the one who has "power ample enough to do good" and to enable them to "safely rest in the protection of him to whose will are subject all the harmful things which, whatever their source, we may fear." No deeper source of comfort and security can be imagined.

For Calvin, providence means "not that by which God idly observes from heaven what takes place on earth, but that by which, as keeper of the keys, he governs all events. Thus it pertains no less to his hands than to his eyes" (sec.4). To put it more succinctly, not only is the eye of God *over* history but the hand of God is *in* history.

Calvin distinguishes "general" and "special" providence. General providence means God's care over all God's work. This "universal providence" embraces what we would call the laws of nature. They are dependable. When a ball is thrown in the air, we can believe it will fall back to the ground due to the law of gravity. These "laws of nature" are not "suspended," willy-nilly.

God's "special providence" is God's direction of the individual (secs. 5, 6). Using numerous texts from Scripture, Calvin argues that humans cannot act or speak except as God wills and that "nothing at all in the world is undertaken without [God's] determination" (sec. 6). God's providence regulates natural occurrences such as powers of procreation and nourishment among humans, leading Calvin to conclude that God's "general providence not only flourishes among creatures so as to continue the order of nature, but is by his wonderful plan adapted to a definite and proper end" (sec. 7). This comprehensive view of providence Calvin maintains is not a Stoic belief in fate (sec. 8), which implies a randomness to life where "whatever will be, will be." Instead, the events of life are regulated by God's providence and purposes for the world and for lives. God's will is primary and the source of all things. We can add that the character of God—who God is—makes the difference here. God is a personal being who relates directly to all God created, including the lives of people. Events are not the fortuitous outworking of "blind fate." They are the expression of God's will and way, the God who is known to us in Scripture. We do not know the true causes of events. But God, "by the bridle of his providence" can turn "every event whatever way he wills" (sec. 9). What some will see as a "contingency" or "fate" or "chance," the eye of faith "recognizes to have been a secret impulse from God."

The doctrine of providence brings great benefits to Christian believers. Calvin notes three things about the ways of God. First, "God's providence must be considered with regard to the future as well as the past" (1.17.1; discussion in secs. 3–5). Second, "God's providence is "the determinative principle of all things in such a way that sometimes it works through an intermediary, sometimes without an intermediary, sometimes contrary to every intermediary." This means that, from the human perspective, life is "wide open." Any event or person or situation can be a means God uses to accomplish God's providential purposes. God may use a *means* as an "intermediary." Or, sometimes, God may work in such a direct way that believers are not aware of any intermediary; events seem like a direct act of God. Then, too, there are times when God's providential purposes are carried out in ways we can never expect. They seem to emerge in ways appearing contrary to any means or intermediary we could imagine. So, we never know. We never know when or where or how God's purposes may develop—in ways unknown to us.

Third, Calvin also notes that God's providence reveals God's concern for the "whole human race" but "especially his vigilance in ruling the church, which he deigns to watch more closely." God's will and purposes for the church are at work in history. It is in and through the church as the people of God that God's providence is especially to be recognized and experienced. Despite the times and situations when God's providence seems hidden to us, we should believe that "God always has the best reason for his plan." Even when violent storms arise and a "gloomy mist is cast over our eyes, thunder strikes our ears and all our senses are benumbed with fright, everything seems to us to be confused and mixed up; but all the while a constant quiet and serenity ever remain in heaven." God directs all such things, even the "disturbances in the world" to a "right end."

While God's rule will be observed, we are not always able to understand it. God's providence is not "automatic" for Christian believers. Calvin said that "in the law and the gospel are comprehended mysteries which tower far above the reach of our senses" (sec. 2). Indeed, God's "wonderful method of governing the universe is rightly called an abyss, because while it is hidden from us, we ought reverently to adore it."

There is comfort in God's providence. But God's providence does not relieve believers from responsibility (sec. 3). We cannot blame our wickedness or adversities on God. God's providence does not excuse us from prudence in living. God has given us means to use for the preservation of our lives; and we should use them (sec. 4). Said Calvin, "God's providence does not always meet us in its naked form, but God in a sense clothes it with the means employed." Neither does God's providence excuse our wickedness. Calvin's analogy is that, while a corpse has a stench, brought out and made worse by the rays of the sun, "yet no one for this reason says that the rays stink" (sec. 5). Since the guilt of evil is in a wicked person, "what reason is there to think that God contracts any defilement, if he uses his service for his own purpose?" The fault for evil is in us; not in God's providence.

Meditating on the ways of God's providence brings happiness to believers (secs. 6–11). It is a comfort to believers to realize that "nothing takes place by chance" so that we can look to God as the "principal cause of things," even as God may also use "secondary causes in their proper place" (sec. 6). God's providence meets us in prosperity (sec. 7). It provides gratitude for prosperity, patience in adversity (sec. 8), and freedom from worry about the future (secs. 10–11). All together, "gratitude of mind for the favorable outcome of things, patience in adversity, and also incredible freedom from worry about the future all necessarily follow upon this knowledge" (sec. 7). "Never-failing assurance" comes from knowing that "when the world appears to be aimlessly tumbled about, the Lord is everywhere at work" and from trusting that God's work will be for our welfare" (sec. 11). Believers can be strengthened through remembering and meditating on God's providence. Indeed, "ignorance of providence is the ultimate of all miseries; the highest blessedness lies in the knowledge of it."

Calvin's views of providence ran up against objections (secs. 12–14). One was that Scripture speaks of God's "repenting" (Genesis 6:6; 1 Samuel 15:11; Jeremiah 18:8). So it looks as if "the plan of God does not stand firm and sure, but is subject to change in response to the disposition of things below" (sec. 12). Calvin's response is that Scripture uses this language of God's "repentance" to allow for our human understanding, speaking of God in human terms (sec. 13). This is another example of accommodation. The description of God we can understand must be "accommodated to our capacity so that we may understand it." So God is represented to us in these instances "not as he is in himself, but as he seems to us." What appears to us as God's changing the divine mind or "repenting" is what things look like from our human perspective. God's eternal plan is being carried out, "uninterrupted," however "sudden the variation may appear" to human eyes.

Calvin ends Book I of the *Institutes* (1.18) by maintaining that "God does whatever he wills" (sec. 1; cf. Psalm 115:3). There is no distinction between God's "willing" and God's "permission." It is God's will that comes to pass in all things, even as the activities of Satan and evil take place (sec. 2). Yet all is according to God's will, which is "the cause of all things." Indeed, the most hideous example of evil is the death of Jesus Christ. Yet, said Calvin, "unless Christ had been crucified according to God's will, whence would we have redemption?" (sec. 3; cf. Acts 4:28). God is not the author of evil; humans are responsible. God "accomplishes through the wicked what he has decreed by his secret judgment," even as the wicked "are not excusable" (sec. 4). While God's will is a cause, humans themselves act and carry the responsibility. While these views may seem difficult, Calvin enjoins that "our wisdom ought to be nothing else than to embrace with humble teachableness, and at least without finding fault, whatever is taught in Sacred Scripture" (sec. 4). Even in the face of evil and wickedness, believers trust the Creator God of Scripture.

8

BOOK II

The Knowledge of God the Redeemer in Christ, First Disclosed to the Fathers under the Law, and Then to Us in the Gospel

IN BOOK II, CALVIN focuses on the human condition after the fall into sin and the nature of sinful humans, especially in regard to "free will." He explores the Law of God, given to provide hope of salvation, the differences between the Old and New Testaments, and then Jesus Christ. Calvin's Christology or doctrine of Christ is a central part of his theology because it is through the person and work of Jesus Christ that God's purposes of salvation are carried out.

KNOWLEDGE OF OURSELVES (2.1–3)

After discussing the knowledge of God the Creator, Calvin turns to the knowledge of ourselves. This is the second portion of his early statement that true wisdom consists of the knowledge of God and knowledge of ourselves (1.1.1).

True self-knowledge is recognizing "what we were given at creation and how generously God continues his favor toward us" (2.1.1). So we are "ever dependent on him." This sets a most basic dimension of the divine/human relationship. We continue to depend on the God who created and sustains us.

But second, we need to recognize "our miserable condition after Adam's fall." This deflates all human boasting and all self-assurance. It overwhelms us with shame. Humans created in the image of God (Gen 1:27) stand in starkest contrast to the "sorry spectacle of our foulness and dishonor," making us displeased with ourselves. It also bends us to true humility and to a zeal to seek God so the good things that have been lost may be recovered.

The self-knowledge we gain from God's truth strips us of all confidence in our own abilities. We are, by nature, those who seek to be flattered, motivated by "blind self-love" (sec. 2). While we may think we can know ourselves by human standards, if the standard of God's judgment is used, we find ourselves driven to utter dejection and powerlessness with nothing in ourselves to direct our lives aright (sec. 3). Humans were created to meditate on divine worship and the future life. But instead, we are in "extreme confusion," unable to carry out our responsibilities to our Creator. We are not the people we should be.

THE RUIN OF THE RACE (2.1.4–7)

The sorry situation of humanity is attributed to the sin of Adam that is characterized by unfaithfulness. The glories of the Garden of Eden, given to Adam and Eve (Genesis 1–2) were lost through disobedience to God's word (Genesis 3) and to the human pride that was the "beginning of all evils" (sec. 4). "Unfaithfulness," says Calvin, was "the root of the Fall." Ambition, pride, and ungratefulness arose as humans rejected the authority of their maker as humans—represented by Adam—"disbelieved in God's Word."

Estrangement from God brought death to the soul of Adam and, in accord with the teachings of the Christian church, this "consigned his race to ruin" by this rebellion against God (sec. 5). This is called "original sin." Humans are sinful in their origins as human beings. Whether one reads the story of Adam and Eve literally or figuratively, the theological point is that humans are now, by nature, sinful people. We are cut off from the relationship of love and trust God intended in the creation. The fault of this sin is our own as the results of original sin take shape in the lives of each of us as we ourselves become sinners. This is an "inherited corruption," which the Psalmist confessed: "Indeed, I was born guilty, a sinner when my mother conceived me" (Ps 51:5). For Calvin, "all of us, who have descended from impure seed, are born infected with the contagion of sin."

The figure of "Adam" is considered the progenitor of the human race, the first created human. However this is understood, the main theological emphasis in Calvin's view is that Adam was also "the root of human nature" (sec. 6). The "infection" of Adam's sin "spread from him to all his descendants." We all are sinners by nature. Therefore "in his corruption mankind deserved to be vitiated" (destroyed). The whole of the human race has been infected with sin. This has broken our relationship with our Creator, cracked the "image of God" in which we were created (Gen 1:27). The ruin into which Adam plunged the race can ultimately only be redeemed by the "second Adam" (see Rom 5:12–21), Jesus Christ. Calvin wrote: "Adam, implicating us in his ruin, destroyed us with himself; but Christ restores us to salvation by his grace."

ORIGINAL SIN (2.1.8–11)

Adam in the Garden received the gifts of God intended to be conferred on the whole human race. But "when he lost the gifts received," Adam "lost them not only for himself but for us all" (sec. 7). Humans now have inherited a corrupted nature, a "hereditary depravity and corruption of our nature," spread throughout our whole souls—our whole selves—and making us liable to God's judgment and wrath (sec. 8). We are "justly condemned" before God, "to whom nothing is acceptable but righteousness, innocence, and purity." We are "entangled in the curse."

As St. Augustine indicated, we are affected by original sin and we all sin by our own actions as well. Our envelopment in original sin "continually bears new fruits—the works of the flesh." So original sin means not only a lack of being the people we should be under God. It is also a power and energy that works away from God. The term "concupiscence" (strong desire) is used to indicate this desire for the evil that stands opposed to God. This power affects the whole person. Whatever is in humans, "[f]rom the understanding to the will, from the soul even to the flesh, has been defiled and crammed with this concupiscence," said Calvin; "or, to put it more briefly, the whole man is of himself nothing but concupiscence."

This sin overturns the whole person. Humanity's corrupt nature means "the mind is given over to blindness and the heart to depravity" (sec. 9). Humans are in need of a complete, new nature. As it is, the whole person is "overwhelmed—as by a deluge—from head to foot, so that no part is immune from sin and all that proceeds from him is to be imputed to sin" (see Rom. 8:6, 7). Our corruption and depravity affect the whole of our lives (sometimes called "total depravity"). Our sinful condition does not reflect on God's handiwork but our own guilt (secs. 10, 11).

CORRUPTION OF THE WILL (2.2)

Philosophers have asserted the freedom of the will, the ability of the will to choose either "virtues" or "vices" (secs. 2, 3). Even some theologians from the church's history have upheld "free decision of choice" (sec. 4), that humans have a "self-power" to choose good or evil, as if humanity "still remained upright" (sec. 4; cf.5–11). But this viewpoint is to rob God of God's honor (sec. 10–11), said Calvin. Humility is the proper attitude before God (sec. 11).

It is true that the "supernatural gifts" God has given are destroyed by original sin—the gifts of faith, love of God, charity toward neighbors. The natural gifts God has given humans—reason and the will—are corrupted by sin. But still, said Calvin, there is enough of reason remaining so that humans are distinguished from the beasts of nature (secs. 12, 13). Indeed, humans may participate in the arts and sciences, seeing science as God's gift. For "if we regard the Spirit of God as the sole fountain of truth, we shall neither reject the truth itself, nor despise it wherever it shall appear, unless we wish to dishonor the Spirit of God" (secs. 14–16). These good gifts of God, which, despite human sinfulness, can still be used and enjoyed are the "general grace of God" (sec. 17; sometimes called "common grace"). Followers of Calvin have often been vigorous participants in the life of society, including practitioners of arts and sciences, as an expression of this "general grace of God," which enables the life of humanity to be blessed with gifts to enhance human well-being.

Yet, "spiritual insight" is not so easily ascertained. This consists of: 1) knowing God (sec. 18); 2) knowing God's parental favor on our behalf (our salvation; secs. 19–21); and knowing how to live our lives according to the rule of God's law (secs. 22–25). But humans are spiritually blind (sec. 19; John 1:4–5). The way to God's kingdom is possible only for those whose minds have "been made new by the illumination of the Holy Spirit" (sec. 20). Without the Spirit, all is darkness (sec. 21). We can have no right knowledge of God by ourselves and our reason (sec. 22–24). Indeed, "Augustine so recognizes this inability of the reason to understand the things of God that he deems the grace of illumination no less necessary for our minds than the light of the sun for our eyes" (sec. 25).

In short, humans have no ability to will the good, when it comes to being able to "choose" to obey and follow God (sec. 26). Humans need the work of the Holy Spirit, which comes "not from nature but from regeneration" (sec. 27).

CONVERSION OF THE CORRUPT WILL (2.3–5)

The Scriptures are clear, says Calvin, that humans must be reborn (John 3:3), for they are "flesh" (3:6). This "rebirth" comes from the Holy Spirit. Yet, humans have "nothing of the Spirit . . . except through regeneration" (2.3.1). Sin affects our minds and desires (Eph 4:22, 23); all our thoughts are perverse. Our hearts are devious and perverse (Jer 17:9; sec. 2) and "all these wicked traits appear in every person," said Calvin. While God restrains human perversity (sec. 3), it is not purged from our nature. The "universal condition" is "human depravity" (sec. 4).

This is a genuine—and dire!—predicament for humans. For "because of the bondage of sin by which the will is held bound, it cannot move toward good, much less apply itself thereto; for a movement of this sort is the beginning of conversion to God, which in Scripture is ascribed entirely to

God's grace" (sec. 5). In the fallen state of sin, the human will is corrupted by sin and cannot will to do the "good"—or to seek after God. In the fallen state of sin, the human will remains eagerly inclined to sin. To capsulize it, Calvin quotes St. Bernard (1090–1153) to say that to will is human; to will ill is of the corrupt nature; while to will well is of grace.

Humans sin of necessity—that is, humans necessarily act according to their natures. If the nature of humans is to be sinful, then "by necessity" (acting according to their natures), they sin. But while humans sin of necessity, they do so without compulsion. That is, they sin willingly. They sin according to the choices of their wills. If the human will is bound to the power of sin, then the choices the will makes will be sinful choices. But the (sinful) choices will be made "freely," that is they will be choices made in accord with the nature of their wills. Humans sin of necessity but without compulsion (sec. 5).

The worst effect of the corrupted will is that humans cannot save themselves. They cannot "choose" to come to God in obedience and love because their sinful nature. So humans are in need of a "divine grace," which "corrects and cures the corruption of nature" (sec. 6). Given human nature as bound in sin, if saving or "salvation" is to occur, God must be the one to do it. Humans cannot lift themselves up by their own bootstraps to get out of the predicament of sin or to change their own sinful natures.

"Everything good in the will is the work of grace alone," says Calvin. God in Jesus Christ "sweeps away everything of our common nature" and by God's pure grace, provides a salvation that is "a free gift" (Eph 2:5). For "the beginning of every good is from the second creation, which we attain in Christ." The "first impulse" in providing salvation and eternal life "belongs to God." In the Old Testament, God had promised the prophet Ezekiel: "A new heart

I will give you, and a new spirit I will put within you . . . and make you follow my statutes and be careful to observe my ordinances" (Ezek 36:26, 27). A new heart and spirit could not be generated by the prophet himself—or any sinner. These are the gift of God. As Calvin said, "Who shall say that the infirmity of the human will is strengthened by his help in order that it may aspire effectively to the choice of good, when it must rather be wholly transformed and renewed?" The transformation that takes place in being "reborn" or conversion to God's will and ways for life means the sinful nature must be "created anew; not meaning that the will now begins to exist, but that it is changed from an evil to a good will." This is God's pure grace. "Regeneration" or the "new birth" or "new life," says Calvin, is "the beginning of the spiritual life." We not only praise God for our salvation, we recognize that we receive it as a gift. We are the "sheep" of God's "pasture" (Ps 100:3), receiving what God has given. There is "not a whit" (nothing) for humans to glory in, "for the whole of salvation comes from God."

This decisive perspective leads Calvin to reject views of salvation that include elements of human "cooperation" with grace (sec. 7). Calvin follows Augustine in seeing God's grace as prior to all things, including any human "merit" or good works that may result from faith in Jesus Christ. It is in the elect of God, those to whom God has chosen to give the gift of salvation, that the Holy Spirit brings the grace of regeneration, new life, or conversion—all from God's "good pleasure by which we were chosen before the creation of the world [Eph 1:4]" (sec. 8). Conversion is "the creation of a new spirit and a new heart," which is fully and completely the work of God, not of us in any way. This is established throughout by the prayers in Scripture (sec. 9).

This emphasis on salvation as completely the work of God was to strike a distinctive position for Calvin in the midst of debates about salvation during and after the Reformation. From beginning to end, salvation is to ascribed to the work of God's Spirit. Faith in Jesus Christ is established by the Spirit, a new "heart" and "will" is given to those who receive the gift of faith. Throughout their lives as God multiplies grace in their lives, Christian believers are held in faith and given the gift of "perseverance" by God's Spirit (sec. 11; "confirming us to perseverance," sec. 6). Calvin believed the Scriptures taught that grace is the "cause of everything" (sec. 12).

Calvin looks to Augustine who put the conditions of humanity in succinct form:

> Adam: *posse, sed non velle*
>
> Adam was able, but not willing to persist in good
>
> We: *posse velle* (after grace)
>
> After God's grace, believers in Christ are able to will to persist in good
>
> Three stages:
>
> *Posse non peccare* (before the fall)
>
> Humans were able not to sin
>
> *Non posse non peccare* (after the fall)
>
> Humans are not able not to sin
>
> *Non posse peccare* (in grace)
>
> Humans in grace (in heaven; in glory) are not able to sin.[1]

---

1. This schema appears in Battles and Walchenbach, *Analysis*, 104, for *Institutes* 2.3.13. To continue the pattern, Augustine also indicated that believers in Christ here on earth are by God's grace, *posse non peccare*, able not to sin. These understandings were particularly important in Augustine's controversy with the Pelagius who advocated complete "free will" so humans can "will" their salvation. Semi-Pelagianism emphasized the combination of free will and God's grace with the initial step toward salvation taken by unaided free will with all else being the gift of God. See the chart in Battles and

As Augustine put it, "Grace alone brings about every good work in us" (sec. 13). For Calvin and Augustine, "the will is not taken away by grace, but is changed from evil into good, and helped when it is good" (sec. 14). All this is by God's will, carried out by the work of the Holy Spirit. Regeneration by the Spirit makes humans a "new creation" in Jesus Christ (2 Cor 5:16–21). This salvation and reconciliation, which features forgiveness of sins (Col 1:14) and peace with God (Rom 5:1), brings freedom (Gal 5:1). Calvin affirms Augustine's teachings that "the human will does not obtain grace by freedom, but obtains freedom by grace" (sec. 14). Put succinctly: "Except through grace the will can neither be converted to God nor abide in God; and whatever it can do it is able to do only through grace."

So Calvin's (and Augustine's) emphasis is on God's work in converting a sinner to being a new creation, a believer in Jesus Christ. Humans cannot do this by their own powers, since they do not have "free will." The term "free will" does not mean we cannot make choices in life—such as whether to pick up a pencil or to go to a store. These things we could call matters of "free choice" or "liberty of choice." Humans can make choices. We are not puppets. But theologically, the human will is not free to choose the good—or to believe the gospel message of Jesus Christ—because the will is captive to sin. Humans do not have, according to Calvin, "choice of judgment and inclination of will that are free." That is, we will not make a judgment to choose to have faith in Christ because the inclination of our will is to sin rather than to receive or accept God's message of love and grace in Christ (see 2.4.8; cf. the argument about free will in 2.5).

Walchenbach, *Analysis*, 102. On the controversies and these viewpoints, see McKim, *Theological Turning Points*, chaps. 4, 5.

REDEMPTION IN CHRIST (2.6)

The human situation in and of itself is hopeless. While God has been revealed in nature—"this magnificent theater of heaven and earth" (sec. 1)—humans sin and cannot come to a true knowledge of God the Creator. For "all our senses have become perverted" and "we wickedly defraud God of his glory." What we need is faith, faith that is focused on "God our Father in Christ." Calvin quotes the apostle Paul: "Since in the wisdom of God the world did not know God through wisdom, it pleased God through the folly of preaching to save those who believe" (1 Cor 1:21). Our only means for salvation from sin is through the cross of Jesus Christ, who is the mediator between God and humanity.

Throughout the Old Testament, argues Calvin, "the blessed and happy state of the church always had its foundation in the person of Christ" (sec. 2). The people of God in the Old Testament began with a covenant with Abraham. He believed God's covenant promise by faith that through him, all the peoples of the earth would be blessed (Gen. 12:3). From Abraham, the people of Israel was established. God promised salvation to come through the line of Abraham's offspring, David. It was through this kingdom of David that "redemption and eternal salvation depended" (sec. 3; (see Isa 55:3-4; Jer 23:5-6). The faith and hope of the Old Covenant rested in the promise of God that salvation would come—which it has, in David's descendent, Jesus Christ.

Calvin said that "God would be through the hand of Christ the deliverer of the church" (sec. 4). Christ is the One through whom we know God. For "unless God confronts us in Christ, we cannot come to know that we are saved." Jesus Christ is God's supreme example of accommodation. Calvin cites the early church theologian Irenaeus that "the Father himself infinite, becomes finite in the Son, for he has accommodated himself to our little measure, lest our minds be overwhelmed by the immensity of his glory." In short, "God is comprehended in Christ alone." "From the beginning of the world," Christ had been "set before all the elect that they should look unto him and put their trust in him."

THE LAW OF GOD (2.7–8)

It is through Jesus Christ, who is the fulfillment of God's covenant promises that salvation comes into the world. After the promise to Abraham, God established the law for the people of Israel. This included the moral law, notably the Ten Commandments (Exod 20:1–17), which "set forth a godly and righteous rule of living" (2.7.1). There was also the ceremonial law, where the true purpose of the ceremonies and sacrifices God required was to lift the minds of the worshipers higher. The law's purpose was a purpose of God's grace, to point the people toward the ultimate coming of Christ. God wanted to adopt Israel to be a "priestly kingdom unto God" (Exod 19:6) and to lift the people's eyes toward the coming of the Mediator, Jesus Christ.

God's law contained a promise. The law was given through Moses and God founded a kingdom through the family of David, from whom God's Mediator, Jesus Christ, emerged. So Christ is "set before the eyes of the ancient folk as in a double mirror" (sec. 2). The movement was from the daily worship sacrifices, required in the law, to the single sacrifice of Jesus Christ to remove sin. Christ is the "fulfillment or end of the law" (cf. Rom 10:4).

When we examine our lives in light of the moral law of God, we find that we cannot obey the law. We disobey and fall short of how God wants us to live. This makes us inexcusable before God. When we look at the law, "we discern in the law only the most immediate death" (sec. 3).

So we cannot reach a blessed state by obeying the law. Yet there is a good purpose to the law. We find that "God, out of his free goodness, shall receive us without looking at our works, and we in faith embrace that same goodness held forth to us by the gospel" (sec. 4). Calvin will take up God's acceptance of us through the gospel when he discusses justification by faith (3.11.1–7). No one—even the greatest saint—is without concupiscence (2.7.5) No human sinner has—or can—fulfill the law of God.

Calvin sees the first function of the law of God to be to show us God's righteousness and our sinfulness. Self-deception and pride cannot be sustained (sec. 6). The law is like a mirror for "in it we contemplated our weakness, then the iniquity arising from this, and finally the curse coming from both—just as a mirror shows us the spots on our face" (sec. 7). This is the sinner's downfall. The law "can only accuse, condemn, and destroy" us and all people (sec. 8). This leads us, as Augustine said, "to flee to grace" (sec. 9).

A second use of the moral law in Calvin's view is that it restrains human sin (secs. 10–11). The law protects a community from unjust persons by leading them to "hold inside the depravity that otherwise they would wantonly have indulged" (sec. 10). The law of God helps to make it possible for society to function since it deters lawlessness by fear (sec. 11).

But the third and "principal use" of the law and its "proper purpose" is what the law does for Christian believers. The law helps believers "learn more thoroughly each day the nature of the Lord's will to which they aspire, and to confirm them in the understanding of it" (sec. 12). The law of God is a guide for Christian living. God has "accommodated" God's self to God's people by instructing them toward "a purer knowledge of the divine will." The law can exhort believers to obedience and draw them back from "the slippery path of transgression." So for Christian believers, the law is "not now acting toward us as a rigorous enforcement officer who is not satisfied unless the requirements are met" (sec. 13). Rather, "the law points out the goal toward which throughout life we are to strive." This is the guidance Christians need—what "shape" should obedient lives take? The answer is: follow God's law to know what God's will is for us. This is our goal and "if we fail not in this struggle, it is well. Indeed, this whole life is a race [cf. 1 Cor 9:24–26]," says Calvin. God has given us the help we need for knowing how to live in ways that are pleasing to God. The law of God is a gift (see Psalm 119).

God's law no longer condemns us since Christ has liberated us from the condemnation of the law (secs. 14–17). Those who follow Christ do not follow the ceremonial law because Christ has liberated us from its use and blotted out all that stood against us (Heb 9:15; Col 2:14; sec. 16).

Calvin goes on to explain the moral law of God as expressed in the Ten Commandments (2.8). In them, we learn that we are to reverence God's righteousness and owe to God the debt of obedience (sec. 4). Jesus Christ is the "best interpreter" of the meaning of the law (sec. 7). The ways rightly to understand the law involve first, with each of the Commandments, to ponder why it was given to us (sec. 8). For example, with the First Commandment (Exod 20:2–3; Deut 6:4–5), the intention is that "God alone is to be worshiped." Thus, we are to understand that "true piety—namely, the worship of his divinity—is pleasing to God; and that he abominates impiety." This is the positive precept that the commandment contains. But then, says Calvin, we also need to understand what the commandment is speaking against—in this case, what it is that displeases God. This became an interpretive principle: there are two sides to every commandment. When something is commanded, its opposite is prohibited; when something is prohibited, its opposite is commanded.

This led Calvin to interpret the Ten Commandments as more than what the words alone say at face value. When both a commandment and prohibition are given (sec. 9), we are to understand what is directed for us in each commandment. It is not enough simply to try to avoid some vice. We must also ask what God is expecting us to do. As an illustration, Calvin said: "In this commandment, 'You shall not kill,' men's common sense will see only that we must abstain from wronging anyone or desiring to do so. Besides this, it contains, I say, the requirement that we give our neighbor's life all the help we can." We are to exercise the "duties of love" to preserve the lives of others.

There are two tables to the Law in the Ten Commandments. Together they convey "the whole of righteousness" (sec. 11). The first part (commandments 1–4) contains "those duties of religion which particularly concern the worship of [God's] majesty; the second (commandments 6–10), to the duties of love that have to do with men." The first table instructs us in worship and piety; in the second table, we find how we ought to "conduct ourselves in human society."

Calvin follows these principles for interpretation of the Commandments with a detailed exposition of the individual commandments (2.8.13–50). Through these, one finds the principles Calvin enumerated carried out. They repay reading to see the theological and ethical concerns Calvin highlights. The moral law can serve as a guide for Christian believers to know God's will and provide help in understanding what to avoid and what to do, what is displeasing to God and what God desires. So a lively concern for obeying God's law is a major part of the Christian life.

The Ten Commandments are prefaced with the reminder of who God is and what God has done: "I am the Lord your God, who brought you out of the land of Egypt, out of the house of slavery" (Exod 20:2). The people of Israel were to obey the law of God in gratitude and thanksgiving to the God who had liberated them from slavery in Egypt. God's deliverance of the people was an act of God's grace. Their obedience to God's law, as God's covenant people, expresses their thankfulness for the "marvelous and everlastingly memorable greatness" God had given, the "benefits" God gave the people (sec. 15). Grace precedes law, including obedience in relation to the law of God. Christians obey the law of God in gratitude for the grace given now in Jesus Christ.

At the end, Calvin discusses the sum of the law (2.8.51). He says the "purpose of the whole law" is the "fulfillment of righteousness to form human life to the archetype of divine purity." If humans obey the law of God, they will express the image of God in which they are created in their own lives. Calvin cites the relevant biblical verses: "That we should love the Lord God with all our heart, with all our soul, and with all our strength" [Deut 6:5; cf. 11:13] "and our neighbor as ourselves" [Lev 19:18; cf. Matt 22:37, 39] and says they mean "our soul should be entirely filled with the love of God. From this will flow directly the love of neighbor." To put it succinctly: "Here is true piety, from which love is derived." In the commandments of the law we find "all the duties of piety and love."

These impulses to show love to others, highlighted in the Ten Commandments and as part of Jesus' own summary of the law (Matt 7:12; cf. Gal 5:14), go counter to human instincts. For Calvin humans were "born in such a state that they are all too much inclined to self-love" (sec. 54). But we keep the commandments when we transfer the emotion of love that we naturally feel for ourselves, toward others. "The emotion of love," says Calvin, "which out of natural depravity commonly resides within ourselves, must now be extended to another, that we may be ready to benefit our neighbor with no less eagerness, ardor, and care than ourselves."

To the question of "Who is my neighbor?" posed to Jesus, Calvin responds with what we can call a "universal ethic." He wrote that, in his parable of the Good Samaritan, Christ showed that "the term 'neighbor' includes even the most remote person [Luke 10:36]" and that "we are not expected to limit the precept of love to those in close relationships" (sec. 55). Calvin went on:

> I say: we ought to embrace the whole human race without exception in a single feeling of love; here there is no distinction between barbarian and Greek, worthy and unworthy, friend and enemy, since all should be contemplated in God, not in themselves ... Therefore, if we rightly direct our love, we must first turn our eyes not to man, the sight of whom would more often engender hate than love, but to God, who bids us extend to all men the love we bear to him, that this may be an unchanging principle: whatever the character of the man, we must yet love him because we love God (sec. 55).

Love is extended to others—to all others. None of the artificial distinctions with which we live—race, gender, nationality, economic location—or anything else limit our love. This love is grounded in our love of God. We love others because God first loved us (1 John 4:19).

OLD AND NEW TESTAMENTS (2.9–11)

The love of God has been operative throughout the Old and New Testaments, according to Calvin. For "God of old willed, through expiations and sacrifices, to attest that he was Father, and to set apart for himself a chosen people" (2.9.1). Throughout the history of Israel, through the law and the prophets, God's promise was firm, even as it appeared "indistinct and shadowed." In a broad sense, the "gospel" or "good news" came to those in the Old Testament who were part of the nation of Israel. For these people received, as we read in the Old Testament, "those testimonies of [God's] mercy and fatherly favor" (sec. 2). These are promises, given by God's grace, that have "now been revealed through the appearing of our Savior Christ Jesus" (2 Tim 1:10). In Jesus Christ, "God has fulfilled what he had promised; that the truth of his promises would be realized in the person of the Son." Jesus Christ has "in his flesh accomplished the whole of our salvation." Now "we are sealed with the 'Holy Spirit of promise' [Eph 1:13]" and "we enjoy Christ only as we embrace Christ clad in his own promises" (sec. 3). The law of God "did not supplant the entire law as to bring forward a different way of salvation. Rather, it confirmed and satisfied whatever the law had promise and gave substance to the shadows" (sec. 4). In contrast to Martin Luther, who emphasized the distinction and disjunction of the "law" and "gospel," Calvin emphasized their continuity.

This is seen in Calvin's discussion of the similarity of the Old and New Testaments (2.10). For him, all who were "adopted by God into the company of his people since the beginning of the world were covenanted to him by the same law and by the bond of the same doctrine as obtains among us" (sec. 1).

Covenant was an important concept for Calvin. The various biblical covenants mark God's way of dealing with God's people, beginning with the covenant of promise to Abraham. For Calvin, "the covenant made with all the patriarchs is so much like ours in substance and reality that the two are actually one and the same" (sec. 2). This is because the whole Old Testament, in which the "old covenant" is given, "was established upon the free mercy of God" (sec. 4). This mercy of God is "confirmed by Christ's intercession." In the Christian gospel, preaching proclaims that "sinners are justified apart from their own merit by God's fatherly kindness; and the whole of it is summed up in Christ" (sec. 4). So salvation comes through God's grace in both the Old Covenant and the New Covenant, who is Jesus Christ himself. The salvation revealed in Christ is "the manifestation of the promises that the Lord had formerly made to Abraham and the patriarchs [Luke 1:54–55, 72–73]." In this sense, "the Old Testament always had its end in Christ and in eternal life."

God continually worked through covenant people who received God's promises. This meant for Calvin that, as God's people in the Old Testament "cleaved [clung] to God" by the "illumination of the Word," they "without any doubt . . . entered into God's immortal Kingdom. For theirs was a real participation in God, which cannot be without the blessing of eternal life" (sec. 7). So God's people under the Old Covenant received eternal life. The covenant dimension always there was "I will be your God, and you shall be my people" (Lev 26:12), says Calvin. So "life and salvation and the whole of blessedness are embraced in these words" (sec. 8). This extended the hope of Old Testament believers "to eternity" since they were "comforted not only amid present misfortunes but for the future by the thought that God would never fail them" (sec. 9).

All this, believers received by faith. The "father of all believers [cf. Gen 17:5]" was Abraham. His faith is "set before us as the best model of believing" (sec. 11). Those who came after Abraham, in faith, looked beyond this present life—with all its difficulties—to an eternal, future life (secs. 13–23). For "however the saints were buffeted about, their final end was to be life and salvation" (sec. 18).

While Calvin emphasized the continuity of Old and New Testaments, drawn together by God's covenants and promises, he also describes five differences between the two Testaments. Calvin sees these all as relating to the "dispensation" or ways by which God relates to people, rather than the "substance" or nature of the differences themselves. These are: 1) representation of spiritual blessings by temporal (2.11.1–3); 2) truth in the Old Testament conveyed by images and ceremonies, typifying Christ (secs. 4–6); 3) the Old Testament is literal; the New, spiritual (secs. 7–8); 4) bondage of the Old Testament and freedom of the New (secs. 9–10); and 5) the Old Testament has reference to one nation, the New to all nations (secs. 11–12). But in light of these differences, Calvin maintains that God is constant throughout: God's "constancy shines forth in the fact that he taught the same doctrine to all ages, and has continued to require the same worship of his name that he enjoined from the beginning" (sec. 13). God's change of "the outward form and manner" does not mean God is "subject to change." Rather, God has "accommodated himself to men's capacity, which is varied and changeable."

JESUS CHRIST THE MEDIATOR (2.12–15)

Key to Calvin's Book II are the closing sections on Christology. Calvin has mentioned Jesus Christ, the mediator and savior who brings salvation in fulfillment of God's covenant promises made in the Old Testament (2.7.1–2). The person and work of Christ he considers here constitute the core of Christian faith. Calvin's teachings about the person of Christ are consistent with the church's historic teachings, developed in the early centuries. His views about the work of Christ, particularly his death on the cross as the means of salvation consider Christ's death from different angles, using various images. The Christian church has never believed there is only one "correct" way of understanding or explaining the death of Christ, called the "atonement," and how it brings salvation. Calvin's thought recognizes some of the variety of New Testament images describing the death of Jesus Christ.

Human sin separates humanity from God the creator. Jesus Christ is the eternal Son of God, whom God sent into the world to live and die and be raised again so human sin can be forgiven and reconciliation between God and humans can occur.

The task of Jesus Christ was "to restore us to God's grace as to make of the children of men, children of God" (2.12.2). Christ is the Mediator, the one who stands between God and humanity. For Calvin, as for orthodox Christianity, Jesus Christ is the one person who exists in two natures—a human and a divine nature. For theological reasons, these two elements were absolutely crucial for the church to maintain. The incarnation—God becoming a human—was, for the sake of humanity, to provide for sinful humans what they could not obtain for themselves: forgiveness of sin and reconciliation with God. Only Jesus Christ could make this happen. As Calvin put it, "Who could have done this had not the self-same Son of God become the Son of man, and had not so taken what was ours as to impart what was his to us, and to make what was his by nature ours by grace?" "Ungrudgingly," Jesus "took our nature upon himself to impart to us what was his, and to become both Son of God and Son of man in common with us."

Our Redeemer must be truly God and truly human. Calvin writes that

> it was his task to swallow up death. Who but the Life could do this? It was his task to conquer sin. Who but very Righteousness could do this? It was his task to rout the powers of world and air. Who but a power higher than world and air could do this? Now where does life or righteousness, or lordship and authority of heaven lie but with God alone? Therefore our most merciful God, when he willed that we be redeemed, made himself our Redeemer in the person of his only-begotten Son [cf. Rom 5:8].

So the Mediator must be truly divine and truly human.

Only this Mediator could become obedient on behalf of disobedient humans. Sin came into the world through the disobedience of Adam (Genesis 3), as Calvin has discussed. To be reconciled with God, it was necessary that humans, who by disobedience "had become lost, should by way of remedy counter it with obedience, satisfy God's judgment, and pay the penalties for sin" (sec. 3). Jesus Christ presented himself to satisfy "God's righteous judgment, and, in the same flesh, to pay the penalty that we had deserved." God became a human in Jesus Christ and in his humanity, he sacrificed himself for us to "wipe out our guilt by his act of expiation and appease the Father's righteous wrath." Christ's human and divine natures are both important. For "he coupled human nature with divine that to atone for sin he might submit the weakness of the one to death; and that, wrestling with death by the power of the other nature, he might win victory for us." As a human, Jesus experienced death; as God, he overcame it. Humans receive the benefits of Christ's action. For "our common nature with Christ is the pledge of our fellowship with the Son of God; and clothed with our flesh he vanquished death and sin together that the victory and triumph might be ours." Calvin believed the only purpose of Christ's incarnation was for our redemption (sec. 4). Christ "assumed flesh" so that "he might become a sacrifice and expiation to abolish our sins."

Having defended the full divinity of Jesus Christ as the second person of the Trinity (1.13), Calvin now defends the true humanity of Christ against those who denied it. In the early church, these included the Manichees and Marcionites (2.13.1). The Marcionites, said Calvin, "fancied Christ's body a mere appearance, while the Manichees dreamed that he was endowed with heavenly flesh." He cites a number of New Testament texts that witness to Christ's full humanity and declares that "Christ is clearly declared to be comrade and partner in the same nature with us" (sec. 2). Jesus was "in every respect has been tested as we are, yet without sin" (Heb 4:15). Jesus was like all others humans, except he did not sin. For Calvin, "he is true man but without fault and corruption" (sec. 4). It is through this Mediator, with a human and divine nature, that salvation for sinful humanity is made possible.

There is a duality and unity in Jesus Christ. He had two natures—divine and human—but is one person. The unity of the person of Christ is to be maintained. As Calvin put it, "We affirm his divinity so joined and united with his humanity that each retains its distinctive nature unimpaired, and yet these two natures constitute one Christ" (2.14.1). This is the historic position of the Christian church. We can speak of this unity of the person through what was called in the ancient church the "communication of the properties" (Lat. *communicatio idiomatum*). This is a way of speaking about the two natures of Christ in relation to his one person. It means that what can be said of Christ's divinity can also be said of his humanity and *vice versa*. As Calvin put it, "The Scriptures speak of Christ: they sometimes attribute to him what must be referred solely to his humanity, sometimes what belongs uniquely to his divinity; and sometimes what embraces both natures but fits neither alone. And they so earnestly express this union of the two natures that is in Christ as sometimes to interchange them. This figure of speech is called by the ancient writers 'the communicating of properties'" (2.14.1; cf. secs. 2–3).

Erroneous views about the person of Christ emerge (sec. 4) when the two natures of Christ are considered as fused together (Eutyches) or separated from each other (Nestorius). Calvin upholds the church's orthodox view that "Christ, as he is God and man, consisting of two natures united but not mingled, is our Lord and the true Son of God even according to, but not by reason of, his humanity" (sec. 4). Christ is "the only-begotten Son of God" and "the church's definition stands firm: he is believed to be the Son of God because the Word begotten of the Father before all ages took human nature in a hypostatic union" (sec. 5). The hypostatic union was defined at the Council of Chalcedon (451 AD) to affirm the union of the two natures of Christ in one person. While the two natures of Christ are distinct from each other, they act together in the one person of Jesus Christ. In Calvin's usage, in Scripture, Christ is given "two names: sometimes calling him Son of God, at other times Son of man" (sec. 6). Views that diverge from the church's classic convictions (e.g., Servetus's: secs. 7–8) are to be rejected.

The person of Christ is expressed in the work of Christ (2.15–17). Calvin deals with the work of Christ in three "offices" or actions: Prophet, King, and Priest. In the

Bible, those who were prophets, kings, and priests were all anointed with oil to carry out their work.

Prophet. While God had provided an "unbroken line of prophets," they all anticipated the coming of the Mediator: Jesus Christ. Jesus was "anointed by the Spirit to be herald and witness of the Father's grace" (2.15.2). He brought "perfect doctrine" to make an "end to all prophecies." In the "sum of doctrine" Christ has given to us, "all parts of perfect wisdom are contained." So Christ teaches us the wisdom of God, including God's will.

King. Christ's kingship is spiritual in nature and eternal. Christ "assures the godly of the everlasting preservation of the church, and encourages them to hope, whenever it happens to be oppressed" (sec. 3). For individual believers, Christ's kingship leads us "to hope for blessed immortality" through the protection of Christ. Despite the "harsh and wretched" conditions in which life is lived, Christ's people recognize that "our happiness belongs to the heavenly life!" (sec. 4). For "our King will never leave us destitute, but will provide for our needs until, our warfare ended, we are called to triumph." He provides us with "confidence to struggle fearlessly against the devil, sin, and death" unto glory. Christ the "anointed" (Lat. *Christus*) by God has been given "all power" by the Father so that "he may by the Son's hand govern, nourish, and sustain us, keep us in his care and help us" (sec. 5). Christ is the "Father's deputy" who "has in his possession the whole power of God's dominion." The Father exercises dominion "through his Son." He is king and pastor of the godly; and will carry out judgment against the wicked.

Priest. Christ is "a pure and stainless Mediator" who by his holiness reconciles us to God (2.15.6). Our sin bars our access to God. So an "expiation" or release from sin is necessary. Christ comes forward with a sacrifice and "by the sacrifice of his death he blotted out our own guilt and made satisfaction for our sins [Heb 9:22]." Christ is our High Priest, having made the perfect sacrifice of himself on our behalf. He is "both priest and sacrifice." As our "everlasting intercessor" before God, Christ is our Mediator and "through his pleading we obtain favor." We can "trust in prayer," have peace of conscience, and rely on God's "mercy." We are "surely persuaded that whatever has been consecrated through the Mediator is pleasing to God." Christ's sacrifice for us is once for all, not a continual re-sacrificing of Christ, as done in the Roman Catholic mass.

JESUS CHRIST THE REDEEMER (2.16.1–12; 2.17)

Jesus Christ in his three offices is our Redeemer who acquires salvation for us (sec. 1). He is divinely sent to us. Facing the wrath of God against our sin, and estranged from God (Col 1:21–22), we realize "how miserable and ruinous our condition is apart from Christ" (sec. 2). This leads us to see how much we owe to God's mercy. For Christ has taken "upon himself and suffered the punishment that, from God's righteous judgment, threatened all sinners." Christ has made expiation, satisfaction, and sacrifice to God so we may have peace with God. Despite our sin, God by "pure and freely give love of us" receives us into grace" (sec. 3). God reconciles us "utterly to himself" in Christ, wiping out "all evil in us by the expiation set forth in the death of Christ; that we, who were previously unclean and impure, may show ourselves righteous and holy in his sight."

This love of God was "established and grounded in Christ" "before the foundation of the world" (Eph 1:4, 5). So it is not that God's Son "reconciled us to him that he might now begin to love those whom he had hated. Rather, we have already been reconciled to him who loves us, with whom we were enemies on account of sin" (sec. 4). This will also relate to Calvin's doctrine of election or predestination (see 3.21–24).

The obedience of Jesus Christ, practiced throughout his life, obtains reconciliation with God for us. Among the images Calvin uses for this salvation are redemption, liberation, and salvation. Christ's crucifixion was the form of death through which Christ as an expiatory sacrifice "discharged all satisfaction through his sacrifice" (sec. 6). Christ took the curse of our sin upon himself, redeeming us from the curse of the law of God, which no one can obey. The burden of human sin was laid on Christ and in taking its curse upon himself, "he crushed, broke, and scattered its whole force. Hence faith apprehends an acquittal in the condemnation of Christ, a blessing in his curse." While death held us captive, "Christ, in our stead, gave himself over to its power to deliver us from it" (sec. 7). Christ "tasted death for everyone" [Heb 2:9] and "by dying, he ensured that we would not die, or—which is the same thing—redeemed us to life by his own death." Christ "died for us" (Rom 5:8). This is sometimes called the substitutionary atonement (see 2.17.4). Christ "bore our sins . . . on the tree" [1 Pet 2:24], means that "the burden of condemnation, from which we were freed, was laid upon Christ" (2.17.4). As Calvin said, the cross of Christ which demonstrates God's love for us (1 John 4:10) shows that "nothing might stand in the way of his love toward us—even human sin (2.17.2).

JESUS CHRIST'S RESURRECTION, ASCENSION, AND HEAVENLY INTERCESSION (2.16.13–18)

"On the third day he rose again from the dead" says the Apostles' Creed. In Christ's resurrection, we receive "a new birth into a living hope through the resurrection of Jesus

Christ from the dead" (1 Pet 1:3). In his resurrection, Christ "came forth victor over death, so the victory of our faith over death lies in his resurrection alone" (2.16.13). Through Christ's death, says Calvin, "sin was wiped out and death extinguished; through his resurrection, righteousness was restored and life raised up, so that—thanks to his resurrection—his death manifested its power and efficacy in us." Christ's death and resurrection go together. Christ's resurrection guarantees our own resurrection (see 1 Cor 15:12–16).

Christ "ascended into heaven" by which "he truly inaugurated his Kingdom" (sec. 14). Now Christ's presence is more useful to us, because now he is not confined to an earthly body. Christ is with us in all times and places: his power and energy are "diffused and spread beyond all the bounds of heaven and earth." Christ's "spiritual presence" is always with us. So the church "holds him by faith, but does not see him with the eyes." Christ will execute judgment in the future (sec. 15). Now he is "our constant advocate and intercessor with God" (sec. 16).

The intercessory work of Christ brings not only the consolation of one who does not condemn us (Rom 8:33, 34) but also assures us that our ultimate Judge on the Day of Judgment is also our Redeemer, Jesus Christ. Calvin writes: "Christ as Intercessor will not condemn those whom he has received into his charge and protection. No mean assurance, this—that we shall be brought before no other judgment seat than of our Redeemer, to whom we must look for our salvation" (sec. 18). What a comfort! Our Judge is also our Savior. This removes fear of judgment because God cares for "the consciences of his people, who tremble in dread of judgment."

9

BOOK III

The Way in Which We Receive the Grace of Christ: What Benefits Come to Us from It, and What Effects Follow

BOOK III OF THE *Institutes* features Calvin's rich treatment of the way in which the grace of Christ is received, benefits that come from it, and the Christian life that follows from our redemption.

THE WORK OF THE HOLY SPIRIT (3.1)

The salvation that comes from Jesus Christ is received by faith. It is through "the secret energy of the Spirit, by which we come to enjoy Christ and all his benefits" (3.1.1). The "testimony" or "witness" of the Spirit "seals the cleansing and sacrifice of Christ" in our hearts. The Holy Spirit is "the bond by which Christ effectually unites us to himself." Faith is "the principal work of the Holy Spirit" (sec. 4). By the Spirit, "the promise of salvation penetrates into our minds, a promise that would otherwise only strike the air or beat upon our ears." Faith itself, says Calvin, has "no other source than the Spirit." So the emphasis in faith is on the divine work of the Spirit rather than any human efforts.

FAITH (3.2)

Faith rests on God's Word. Through the Scriptures, the Spirit works to bring us to faith in Jesus Christ. The Word is "like a mirror in which we may contemplate God" (sec. 6). "If you take away the Word," says Calvin, "no faith will then remain." Faith is not only knowing that God exists but especially "knowing what is his will toward us." Faith is "a knowledge of God's will toward us, perceived from his Word."

A fuller definition of faith is "a firm and certain knowledge of God's benevolence toward us, founded upon the truth of the freely given promise in Christ, both revealed to our minds and sealed upon our hearts through the Holy Spirit" (sec. 7). So faith is a form of knowledge—a heart knowledge of God's benevolence or goodness to us. It is personal. It is not simply speculation but is founded on the truth of God's promise in Christ. Faith receives God's promise in Christ, a gift. This promise is assured, making it firm and certain. Faith is a relational knowledge that unites us by faith to Jesus Christ—by the work of the Holy Spirit.

Calvin's definition of faith stresses that "faith consists in assurance rather than in comprehension" (sec. 14). Faith is sure and firm giving us the "constancy of persuasion" (sec. 15). Faith is "a sure confidence in divine benevolence and salvation." It is grounded in God's acts. Faith as "firm conviction" is "relying upon the promises of divine benevolence toward us" (sec. 16). This assurance of faith can preserve us through all conflicts. For "faith ultimately triumphs over those difficulties which besiege and seem to imperil it" (sec. 18).

Book III

Faith maintains its confidence and trust through temptations, fears, and difficulties. As we walk by faith, we walk in union with Christ. Calvin says that "since Christ has been so imparted to you with all his benefits that all his things are made yours, that you are made a member of him, indeed one with him, his righteousness overwhelms your sins; his salvation wipes out your condemnation; with his worthiness he intercedes that your unworthiness may not come before God's sight . . . That condemnation which we of ourselves deserve has been swallowed up by the salvation that is in Christ" (sec. 24). This vital union with Christ allows us to participate in Christ and receives his benefits.

Far from being detached, faith means the closest possible relationship of trust and love for Christ, through the power of the Holy Spirit. Calvin writes: "So Christ is not outside us but dwells within us. Not only does he cleave to us by an indivisible bond of fellowship, but with a wonderful communion, day by day, he grows more and more into one body with us, until he becomes completely one with us" (sec. 24). One's relationship with Jesus Christ could not be deeper or more dynamic. Communion with Jesus Christ by faith is the most personal and lifegiving relationship we can imagine.

In the end, faith does not assure believers of earthly prosperity but rather that "God will never fail" (sec. 28). The "chief assurance of faith rests in the expectation of the life to come, which has been placed beyond doubt through the Word of God." It is God's benevolence that is our "full happiness," no matter what life deals us. For the Christian, the "sum of blessedness" is "the grace of God; for from this fountain every sort of good thing flows unto us."

God's promise of mercy is "the proper goal of faith" (sec. 29) and "there can be no firm condition of faith unless it rests upon God's mercy" (sec. 30). Every promise of God is a "promise of his love" (sec. 32). No wonder that faith, as well as being a knowledge of the "head," is also a knowledge of the "heart." "For the Word of God," said Calvin, "is not received by faith if it flits about in the top of the brain, but when it takes root in the depth of the heart" (sec. 36). This faith sustains us throughout our doubts (sec. 37).

Faith and hope belong together, urges Calvin. For "hope is nothing else than the expectation of those things which faith has believed to have been truly promised by God. Thus, faith believes God to be true, hope awaits the time when his truth shall be manifested" (sec. 42). In short, "faith is the foundation upon which hope rests, hope nourishes and sustains faith." Both faith and hope are grounded in God's mercy. "Hope is nothing but the nourishment and strength of faith" (sec. 43), Calvin maintains.

REPENTANCE (3.3–5)

The faith given to us by the grace of God through the Holy Spirit expresses itself in repentance. For Calvin, "the sum of the gospel is held to consist in repentance and forgiveness of sins [Luke 24:47; Acts 5:31]" (3.3.1). It is important to note that repentance follows faith; repentance is "born of faith." It is not, as in some theologies, that we "repent" and then have faith. Instead, repentance is founded in the gospel. We recognize sin and turn away from it (repentance) as an expression of the faith granted to us in the gospel of Jesus Christ. We cannot repent without knowing we belong to God, said Calvin, "but no one is truly persuaded that he belongs to God unless he has first recognized God's grace" (sec. 2). Repentance is not a "work" we do; it is a sorrow for sin and a walk into newness of life that comes as a response to God's gracious love in Jesus Christ.

There are two parts to repentance: mortification—the sorrow of our souls for our sins (contrition); and vivification—"a desire arising from rebirth" that we begin to live to God (sec. 3). The term "conversion" describes this whole process of repentance and faith (sec. 5). Repentance is turning to God (sec. 6), fearing God (sec. 7), and is regeneration—to "restore in us the image of God that had been disfigured and all but obliterated through Adam's transgression" (sec. 9). In Jesus Christ, we are regenerated to be the people our Creator intended us to be, living in the image of God.

Believers who experience regeneration are still sinners. There remains in the regenerate "a smoldering cinder of evil" that spurs us to commit sin (sec. 10). But, in believers, sin has lost its dominion or power (sec. 11). In believers, "sin ceases only to reign; it does not also cease to dwell in them." In baptism, the guilt of sin is taken away, but traces of sin still remain. Calvin rejected the view of Anabaptists who believed that, after baptism, children of God are "restored to the state of innocence"—like Adam was at creation (sec. 14). Christians are not "perfect," only forgiven. The Holy Spirit is given to believers in Christ to lead us into obedience, "far removed from perfection, we must move steadily forward, and though entangled in vices, daily fight against them." Repentance does not consist of fasting and weeping. It is instead, "the conversion of the entire heart to the Lord" (sec. 17). Christians must devote themselves to repentance "throughout life" (sec. 20) as we continually receive God's mercy and the forgiveness of sins. God's mercy leads us to repent (see Rom 2:4). So repentance is a "singular gift of God" (sec. 21). Calvin rejected various Roman Catholic practices about repentance, confession of sins, forgiveness, indulgences, and purgatory (3.4–5). All these are misinterpretations of Scripture. Confession of sin is simply made to God: it is "the Lord who forgives, forgets, and wipes out, sins, let us confess our sins to him in order to obtain pardon" (3.4.9).

THE CHRISTIAN LIFE (3.6–10)

The purpose of God's regenerating persons with the gift of faith in Jesus Christ is to bring them to obedience to God's will and adopt them into the family of God, the church (Gal 4:5; 2 Pet 1:10). Calvin turns to a "pattern for the conduct of life" (3.6.1), which gives us purpose and direction for Christian living (sec. 2). Christ himself is our "example, whose pattern we ought to express in our life" (sec. 3). Our lives are to "express Christ, the bond of our adoption" since he has "engrafted us into his body." The Christian life is "a doctrine not of the tongue but of life," rooted in "the inmost affection of the heart" (sec. 4). The goal of Christian life is not perfection—because no one could attain that (sec. 5)! We proceed on our journey, daily trying "to make some headway, thought it be slight," with "continuous effort" through "the whole course of life." Our life in faith is always, as the road sign says: "Under Construction."

The sum of the Christian life, according to Calvin, is the denial of ourselves, and the dedication and consecration of ourselves to God in order that we may "think, speak, meditate, and do, nothing except to his glory" (3.7.1). We are not our own (1 Cor 6:19), "we are God's: let his wisdom and will therefore rule all our actions." We are to "apply the whole force" of our abilities "in the service of the Lord" so we "may no longer live but hear Christ living and reigning" within us (Gal 2:20). This is the "denial of self which Christ enjoins with such great earnestness upon his disciples at the outset of their service [cf. Matt 16:24]" (sec. 2).

This self-denial gives us the right attitudes toward others. We must tear out from ourselves "the pestilence of love of strife and love of self" and "call ourselves back to humility" (sec. 4). We remember all our gifts are from God so we live in humility toward ourselves and with "reverence for others." We recognize all the benefits we receive from God "have been entrusted to us on this condition: that they be applied to the common good of the church" and that there be "a liberal and kindly sharing of them with others" (sec. 5). For God has given all the gifts we possess "on condition that they be distributed for our neighbors' benefit [cf. 1 Pet 4:10]." Our "stewardship" is how we use what we have been given for us and "the only right stewardship is that which is tested by the rule of love." Christians look at the image of God in all people so we owe them "all honor and love" (sec. 6). Whomever we meet "who needs your aid, you have no reason to refuse to help him," said Calvin. This is a comprehensive call to Christian care for others.

Key to self-denial before God is to "resign ourselves and all our possessions to the Lord's will, and to yield to him the desires of our hearts to be tamed and subjugated" (sec. 8). We do not greedily strive after riches and honors (sec. 9). But we always look to the Lord so that by God's "guidance we may be led to whatever lot he has provided for us." Permitting every part of our lives to be "governed by God's will" helps us bear all adversities (sec. 10) and to undergo them with "a peaceful and grateful mind."

The life of Jesus Christ on earth was "nothing but a sort of perpetual cross" (3.8.1). As followers of Christ, believers "share Christ's sufferings" to be "led through various tribulations to the same glory [Acts 14:22]." These suffering lead us to trust in God's power as through "the testing of the cross," God brings us into "a deeper knowledge of himself" (sec. 2). We transfer our trust away from ourselves to God, so that we can "rest with a trustful heart in God" and persevere to the end (sec. 3). The cross trains us into patience and obedience (sec. 4). When chastisements come from God (sec. 6) and sufferings (sec. 7), we rest in "the spiritual consolation of God" (sec. 8).

Enduring the cross in this life leads us to "meditate upon the future life" (3.9). We are grateful for our earthly life, as a "gift of God's kindness" (3.9.3). But we also desire the heavenly life, eternal life in the "presence of God," which is "the summit of happiness" (sec. 4). This is a destiny to dream about! Christians do not fear death, says Calvin, and "no one has made progress in the school of Christ who does not joyfully await the day of death and final resurrection" (sec. 5). For, "if believers' eyes are turned to the power of the resurrection, in their hearts the cross of Christ will at last triumph over the devil, flesh, sin, and wicked men" (sec. 6).

In the meantime, we can enjoy the good things of the present life as gifts of God (3.10.1). They can delight us as well as meet our needs (sec. 2). We use what God has given, recognizing all good comes from God and giving "thanks for his kindness toward us" (sec. 3). We have great freedom in our outer life, bearing poverty "peaceably" and "abundance moderately" (sec. 4). We recognize all our earthly possessions are from God, given for our benefit, and for which we will have to account to God (sec. 5). We live, looking to our calling (vocation), the particular kind of life God assigns to us. Our vocation helps "as a sort of sentry post" so we do not "heedlessly wander about throughout life" (sec. 6). It is the Lord's calling that is "in everything the beginning and foundation of well-doing."

Book III

JUSTIFICATION (3.11–18)

After Calvin described regeneration by faith and the Christian life, he goes back to their foundations by considering justification. Calvin describes the theological topics of justification and sanctification as a "double grace" (3.11.1). In justification, we are "reconciled to God through Christ's blamelessness." In sanctification, "by Christ's spirit we may cultivate blamelessness and purity of life." These two are distinct, but related for Calvin. They are the means by which believers are accepted by God in Christ and by which they grow in Christian faith and life. Calvin called justification "the main hinge on which religion turns."

Two elements stand out in justification as God accepts us into favor as righteous persons: "the remission of sins and the imputation of Christ's righteousness" (sec. 2). In Christ, sin is forgiven and the righteousness that belongs to Jesus Christ by virtue of who he was—the sinless, Son of God—is given to us as sinners. We receive this gift of grace by faith, given by the Holy Spirit. The result is a new status before God: we are considered righteous in God's sight because the righteousness of Christ is imputed (imputation) and given to us. God graciously forgives our sin and accepts us into the family of faith (sec. 4). We receive new life (regeneration) and are remade in the image of God (sec. 6; cf. 3.17.5). We are adopted into the family of God (the church; Rom 8:15) and now live in gratitude and obedience.

Faith is the means by which we receive justification. We receive the "indwelling of Christ in our hearts," a "mystical union," says Calvin, so that "Christ, having been made ours, makes us sharers with him in the gifts with which he has been endowed" (sec. 10). In short, we receive Christ's righteousness and he makes us "one with him."

Calvin is careful to indicate that this new life in Christ comes not by a combination of faith and works but by grace through faith (sec. 13; cf. secs. 17–20). In Christ we are "accounted righteous" (Rom 5:19) so that our righteousness is "in Christ's obedience, because the obedience of Christ is reckoned to us as if it were our own" (sec. 23). We do not take confidence in ourselves, sinful as we are. As Augustine put it, we rely solely on God's goodness when, "forgetting our own merits, we embrace Christ's gifts" (see 3.12.8). In justification, we give glory to God, not ourselves (3.13.2). Calvin indicates that faith, through which we receive the grace of justification, is "something merely passive, bringing nothing of ours to the recovering of God's favor but receiving from Christ that which we lack" (3.13.5). We contribute nothing to our righteousness (3.14.6). We are saved by grace, not as "the result of works, so that no one may boast" (see Eph 2:8–9; 3.14.11; cf. secs. 16, 17).

After justification, the place for works done by Christians is as a sign of their new life in Christ. Good works are the "fruits of regeneration as proof of the indwelling of the Holy Spirit" (3.14.19). These works do not earn "merit" before God, they are instead the "gifts of God" to help us recognize God's goodness to us and as "signs of the calling" by which we realize our election (3.14.20; cf. 3.24.4). Scripture says we are not to "grow weary in doing what is right" (Gal 6:9). But the credit for all good works belongs to God: "We are not dividing the credit for good works between God and man, as the Sophists [Roman Catholics] do, but we are preserving it whole, complete, and unimpaired for the Lord" (3.15.3). The doctrine of justification does not do away with good works. Rather "faith and good works must cleave together," with justification not being by works but by faith (3.16.1). For "Christ justifies no one whom he does not at the same time sanctify." Justification and sanctification can be distinguished but not separated. A justified person will be sanctified by God's Spirit, growing in faith—and doing good works. On justification and sanctification, Calvin says that the Lord "bestows both of them at the same time, the one never without the other."

CHRISTIAN FREEDOM (3.19)

The doctrines of justification and sanctification bring a great freedom to the Christian person (3.19). Three parts are important.

First, freedom in Christ means one is free from the law in the sense of trying to keep God's law as a way by which one becomes justified in God's sight. We are not saved by keeping God's law, which we could never do. We are not saved by our "good works." Our freedom is that in justification we "embrace God's mercy alone, turn our attention from ourselves, and look only to Christ" (sec. 2). Salvation by God's grace frees us from needing to try to justify ourselves before God.

Second, this leaves us free to "willingly obey God's will" (sec. 4). Since our consciences are free from trying to keep God's law as a means to justify ourselves before God, now in Christ, we willingly keep God's law, which is an expression of God's will. We are free to obey God's law as a way of showing that we want to love God with all our heart, soul, and might (Deut 6:5). Now our obedience is joyful. We respond to the voice of God to obey and live as God desires. Christian believers hear themselves called with "fatherly gentleness by God" and will "cheerfully and with great eagerness answer, and follow his leading" (sec. 5). We have freedom to obey.

A third part of Christian freedom is in relation to things "indifferent," (Lat. *adiaphora*) that is, practices that may or may not be followed. These are neither "positive" nor "negative." Calvin used examples of eating meat, celebrating holidays, or using church vestments. These are things that may or may not be rightly practiced by Christians; they are "indifferent." Our freedom in Christ means that "we are not bound before God by any religious obligation preventing us from sometimes using them and other times not using them, indifferently" (sec. 7). The point is that "we should use God's gifts for the purpose for which he gave them to us, with no scruple of conscience, no trouble of mind. With such confidence our minds will be at peace with him, and will recognize his liberality toward us" (sec. 8). We are free to use "the good things of God," thanking God for them, and to "praise God in his works."

Our freedom is not granted to us so we can give offense against others or to cause others to stumble and turn away from God's will. We are not to use our freedom "as an opportunity for self-indulgence" (Gal 5:13). Our freedom is given to enable us to care for others, to make us "their servants in all things" (sec. 11). Our freedom is given so we may have "peace with God in our hearts" and so we can live at peace with others. At times we may choose not to use our freedom so the needs of others can be met. If it does not help others, then "we should forego it" (sec. 12). Our freedom in Christ in outward matters has been given so we may "be the more ready for all the duties of love" because "we must at all times seek after love and look toward the edification of our neighbor."

PRAYER (3.20)

Calvin devoted the longest chapter in the *Institutes* to prayer. Prayer is necessary in the Christian life and brings many benefits. In prayer we invoke God's providence and power (sec. 1). This brings "an extraordinary peace and reposes to our consciences. For having disclosed to the Lord

Book III

the necessity that was pressing upon us, we even rest fully in the thought that none of our ills is hid from him who, we are convinced, has both the will and the power to take the best care of us." Prayer is an expression of trust in God.

Calvin discusses four rules of prayer.

1. Pray with reverence (secs. 4–5):
   Prayer is "conversation with God" (sec. 4). It is an "intimate conversation" (sec. 5). We keep focused on God and are moved by God's majesty. We bring before God that which we hope to be in accordance with God's will (1 John 5:14). The Holy Spirit is our "teacher in prayer, to tell us what is right and temper our emotions," even as the Spirit intercedes with God for us (Rom 8:26).

2. Pray from a sincere sense of want, and with penitence (secs. 6–7):
   We pray from a sense of our own insufficiency. We should not pray only out of a sense of duty or just to try to appease God (sec. 6). All times are times when our needs urge us to pray (sec. 7). In prayer, we repent and express our sorrow for our sins, knowing our prayers do not depend on our "worthiness."

3. Pray by abandoning all self-glory and self-assurance (secs. 8–9):
   We put away all self-glory and self-assurance. Our only assurance is we do not need to despair that God will take care of us (sec. 8). We rely on "God's mercy alone" knowing that our plea for God's forgiveness is the most important part of prayer (sec. 9)

4. Pray with confident hope (secs. 11–14):
   In humility, we have "a sure hope that our prayer will be answered" (sec. 11). Repentance and faith go together in prayer. When the saints of God experience

the most unrest and are "almost driven out of their senses," they will pray. Their hope is for "escape and deliverance," taking refuge in God. Through it all, faith is a "guide" and "it is faith that obtains whatever is granted to prayer." A "firm sense of the divine benevolence" is a faith experienced in our hearts. This faith is "grounded in unshaken assurance of hope" (sec. 12). Our assurance in prayer is established in God's promise and command to pray, clearly expressed by the Psalmist: "Call upon me in the day of affliction; I will deliver you, and you shall glorify me" (Ps 50:15), a promise which had "encouraged" the Psalm writer, David (sec. 13). So prayer should be made realizing "how gently God attracts us to himself" (sec. 14). Our prayers do not depend on any merit of ours, "but their whole worth and hope of fulfillment are grounded in God's promises, and depend upon them, so that they need no other support."

In prayer, we seek to conform to God's will. But we may pray to God, no matter how we feel, even when we are in lament or complain against God. Calvin notes that when King David felt that way, "he finds no other solace better than to cast his own sorrows into the bosom of God . . . God tolerates even our stammering and pardons our ignorance whenever something inadvertently escapes us; as indeed without this mercy there would be no freedom to pray" (sec. 16). None of our prayers are "perfect." But they do not need to be. Calvin said "there is no prayer which in justice God would not loathe if he did not overlook the spots with which all are sprinkled." In prayer, we can, with faith and hope, "let it all hang out"!

When we recognize we are not worthy of presenting ourselves to God in prayer, instead of despair, we see that God has "given us his Son, Jesus Christ our Lord, to be our advocate [1 John 2:1] and mediator with him [1 Tim 2:5] by whose guidance we may confidently come to him, and with such an intercessor, trusting nothing we ask in his name will be denied us, as nothing can be denied to him by the Father" (sec. 17). We need "a Mediator, who should appear in our name and bear us upon his shoulders and hold us bound upon his breast so that we are heard in his person" (sec. 18). This is the risen Christ who prays for us and who asks that "all members of Christ's body mutually pray for one another" (sec. 20). All Christian believers have the Son who through the power of his death makes "an everlasting intercession in our behalf [cf. Rom 8:34]."

The form of prayer that God taught through Jesus is the Lord's Prayer, a model prayer for Christians. Calvin expounds each of the phrases in the Prayer (secs. 34–47). His discussion repays careful study. We are not bound to using only the Lord's Prayer or only its words. What is important, is that this prayer summarizes the important parts of prayer. We are free to pray our own prayers and "though the words may be utterly different, yet the sense ought not to vary" (sec. 49). Calvin recommends we should "set apart certain hours" for prayer (sec. 50). In times of adversity and prosperity, we hasten to pray to God "with eager hearts." In all our prayers, we ask that God's will be done. In prayer, we do not try to impose a law on God.

We continue to "persevere in prayer" (sec. 51). God does not always respond to our first requests but answers "in his own time." God promises "to care for us in our troubles, when they have once been laid upon his bosom. And so he will cause us to possess abundance in poverty, and comfort in affliction. For though all things fail us, yet God will never forsake us" (sec. 52). God does not always answer our prayers in "the exact form of our request." But even though God seems "to hold us in suspense," yet "in a marvelous manner shows us our prayers have not been vain." In short, even when God "does not comply with our wishes," God is "still attentive and kindly to our prayers, so that hope relying upon his word will never disappoint us." Believers "need to be sustained by this patience, since they would not long stand unless they relied upon it." In and through the most difficult times, believers have an assurance of hope that God hears and answers prayer. We do not cease to pray. For, as Calvin said, "unless there be in prayer a constancy to persevere, we pray in vain."

ELECTION AND PREDESTINATION (3.21–24)

When the name John Calvin is mentioned, the term "predestination" or "election" often follows. Calvin and the later Calvinism that developed after his death are often perceived as having emphasized a doctrine of predestination that makes humans into puppets or that makes God an arbitrary figure. It is all cast in negative terms.

Near the end of Book III of the *Institutes*, Calvin discussed the biblical doctrine of election and the predestination that accompanies it. It is a capstone, a great "summing up" of what has gone before. Election and predestination are theological explanations of the whole doctrine of redemption. They confess salvation has been the work of God in our lives. They stand as the culmination of what Calvin emphasized as the priority of God and God's initiative in providing justification by faith through the Holy Spirit. This is God's gift. Election or predestination is another way of saying salvation is by God's grace.

It is clear from life that some, but not all people come to a knowledge of God in Jesus Christ and express faith. Calvin says, based on his understanding of Scripture, that this is due to God's eternal election (3.21.1). He believes the Bible makes clear that "our salvation comes about solely from God's mere generosity." This calls us "back to the course of election." To be avoided are "excessive curiosity on one hand" (trying to investigate what God has "left hidden in secret"), and "excessive ingratitude on the other" (neglecting what God has brought into the open). Following Augustine, Calvin said that "we can safely follow Scripture, which proceeds at the pace of a mother stooping to her child, so to speak, so as not to leave us behind in our weakness" (sec. 4). This accommodation by God is to help us rightly understand that God wants us to understand what God has revealed about election and predestination.

Two terms are important. The first is foreknowledge, which means that, for God, "all things always were, and perpetually remain, under his eyes so that to his knowledge there is nothing future or past, but all things are present" (sec. 5). As we would say, because God is outside space and time, everything for God is an "eternal present." God sees all things at once, as "present." This extends "throughout the universe to every creature." So God has foreknowledge of all things.

The second term, predestination, means "God's eternal decree, by which he compacted with himself what he willed to become of each man. For all are not created in equal condition; rather, eternal life is foreordained for some, eternal damnation for others. Therefore, as any man has been created to one or the other of these ends, we speak of him as predestined to life or to death" (sec. 5). Predestination relates to humans.

What Calvin wants to maintain is that God is free to do what God wills; and especially, that God's grace is free. It is given according to God's will. Calvin argued that in the election of the nation of Israel to be God's people, "God has already shown that in his mere generosity he has not been bound by any laws but is free, so that equal apportionment of grace is not to be required of him. The very inequality of his grace proves that it is free" (sec. 6).

God's grace cannot be prescribed by us, telling God to whom to extend grace. God is gathering God's church "from Abraham's children" through the covenant. God has adopted and "predestines for himself those whom he willed" for salvation. This is an expression of God's free grace (sec. 7). God's "elect" are those who receive God's "freely given mercy, without regard to human worth." We see this in God's call to us as a "testimony to election" and in justification, when the gift of faith is given in this life; and eventually when the elect "come into the glory in which the fulfillment of that election lies."

Key to this is that "God has always been free to bestow his grace on whom he wills" (3.22.1). God does not foresee peoples' "merits" and then decide to give them grace. Rather, salvation is by God's grace alone. The way or means by which salvation is received is through faith in Jesus Christ. Calvin calls Jesus Christ "the mirror wherein we must, and without self-deception may, contemplate our own election" (3.24.5). This means that, as we look at Jesus Christ, we see God's loving electing grace (cf. 2.17.1 where Calvin quotes Augustine as saying that "there is no more illustrious example of predestination than the Mediator himself"). God's grace engrafts us into Christ (through justification) and brings us into union and "communion with Christ." When we see and experience this faith in Christ and recognize our union with Christ by the work of the Holy Spirit, we realize our election. We realize our faith in Jesus Christ is not of our own doing. It is the work of God within us, God's election. As the New Testament says: God "chose us in Christ before the foundation of the world to be holy and blameless before him in love. He destined us for adoption as his children through Jesus Christ, according to the good pleasure of his will" (Eph 1:4–5).

So, says Calvin, "the Lord wills that in election we contemplate nothing but his mere goodness" (3.22.9). All sinners deserve God's judgment for the sin that breaks our relationship with God. "Among all the offspring of Adam," said Calvin, "the Heavenly Father found nothing worthy of his election" (3.22.1). So God "turned his eyes upon his Anointed, to choose from that body as members those whom he was to take into the fellowship of life" (sec. 1). No sinner deserves salvation. That God chooses to save some is an act of God's pure grace. For "the whole intent of our election is that we should be to the praise of divine grace [cf. Eph 1:6]" (3.22.3).

Because salvation rests on God's action, "God's firm plan that election may never be shaken will be more stable than the very heavens" (3.22.7). We can believe too that "Christ does not allow any of those whom he has once for all engrafted into his body to perish [John 10:28]" (3.22.7; cf. 3.24.6, 7). Those to whom God has given faith will persevere in their faith. Election is "the mother of faith," said Calvin, meaning our faith does not depend on ourselves (3.22.10). Our faith comes from and is sustained by God's loving election.

Calvin spends a number of pages responding to objections to election and predestination (3.23, 24). He maintains that along with election is also reprobation. This refers to those "whom God passes over, he condemns" (3.23.1; reprobates). This too is done by God's will. God allows some to face the consequences of their sin and not share in eternal life (Rom 9:19–24). Calvin does not say God directly wills their condemnation. But God allows the results of their sin to take their course and this leads to them receiving the "wages of sin," which is death (Rom 6:23). Calvin believed he was following Paul (and Augustine; Rom 9:22) in ascribing to "God the credit for salvation, while he casts the blame for their perdition upon those who out of their own will bring it upon themselves." All humans deserve condemnation because of their sin. Each person sins. God elects to save some, out of mercy. In it all, Calvin maintains God is righteous and free and so cannot be charged with injustice toward the sinner (3.23.2–4). There is no distinction between "God's will" and "God's permission" (3.23.8). Election does not make all admonitions or preaching meaningless. Preaching is the means God uses to make the message of salvation known (3.23.13). So preaching must be carried out so the message of salvation can be made known. These, among Calvin's other responses were attempts to give explanations of the doctrine of election.

In the end, election is a mystery. But since it is God's will, it is not to be judged by an external standard—such as our views about what is "just" or "unjust." Most important is to see election as a source of comfort and hope since it grounds our salvation in God's loving power, rather than our own efforts. The most important personal question in election is: "Do I believe in Jesus Christ?" For it is in him that God's election is focused. We do not speculate about the eternal decrees of God. We look at where God's election is centered: in Jesus Christ. Since he is the means by which we know our election, the question for all persons is: "Do I believe in Jesus Christ?" If one desires to believe in Christ, it is a sign that the Holy Spirit is at work toward establishing faith. If one were living only in sinfulness, without any working of the Holy Spirit, one would have no concern with matters of salvation or the call of Jesus Christ. So as Calvin put it: "Let us therefore embrace Christ, who is graciously offered to us, and comes to meet us. He will reckon us in his flock and enclose us within his fold" (3.24.6). For us, election begins and ends with God's call in Christ. God's election provides us with "the inestimable fruit of comfort" (3.24.4).

THE FINAL RESURRECTION (3.25)

The climax of salvation is eternal life and the "blessed resurrection" (3.25.1). This is the fullest expression of our union with God when, after death, we receive "the fruit of Christ's benefits."

A beautiful statement is when Calvin writes that "Christ rose again that he might have us as companions in the life to come" (sec. 3). Christ's resurrection is a mirror to give us "a firm foundation to support our minds." Christ's resurrection is the basis for "the resurrection of us all" (1 Cor 15:23). His resurrection is the "pledge" of our own. Because he lives, we too shall live. The resurrection of the body is our hope, grounded in Christ's resurrection. For "we arise because Christ arose [1 Cor 15:12ff.]" (sec. 7). In Christ, "death has been swallowed up in victory" (1 Cor 15:54).

Those cut off from God (reprobates) face darkness and torments in hell, the results of their wickedness, metaphorically described in Scripture (Matt 3:12; 22:13 etc.). These images point to "how wretched it is to be cut off from all fellowship with God" (3.25.12).

But the final resurrection, grounded in Christ, brings everlasting blessedness to the righteous, an "eternal happiness" (sec. 10). The righteous in Christ are, in heaven, brought into oneness with God. "Let us remember," said Calvin, "that every sort of happiness is included under this benefit." This eternal blessedness praises God who is "all in all" (1 Cor 15:28; sec. 12).

10

BOOK IV

The External Means or Aids by Which God Invites Us Into the Society of Christ and Holds Us There

From the salvation found in Christ and the "eternal blessedness brought by him" (4.1.1), Calvin moves on to discuss the "outward helps" that "beget and increase faith within us." God has provided aids to help us in our weakness and deposited these in the church. So Book Four considers the church and its sacraments, Baptism and the Lord's Supper, with a concluding chapter on Civil Government.

THE CHURCH (4.1–13)

The church is another example of God's providence and accommodation in helping us in our weakness to "draw near to him" (sec. 1). Pastors, teachers, and sacraments are ways God helps to nourish and nurture those God has gathered together in faith in the church.

It is God alone who knows the true church, those God has elected and called (2 Tim 2:19; sec. 2). The church is "catholic" or "universal" because there is only one church and "all the elect are so united in Christ [cf. Eph 1:22–23] that as they are dependent on one Head, they also grow together into one body, being joined and knit together [cf. Eph 4:16] as are the limbs of a body [Rom 12:5; 1 Cor 10:17; 12:12, 27]." They are made truly one because they live together in one faith, hope, and love, and in the same Spirit of God" (sec. 2). This unity of the church, united by the Holy Spirit with Jesus Christ as its head, is a basic tenet of Calvin's ecclesiology, or view of the church. All else flows from this unity, which is established by God.

The church is "the communion of saints" as the Apostles' Creed says (sec. 3). It is the "society of Christ," the "society of God" where those joined by God's election are united in Christ's love and "cannot but share their benefits with one another." The "visible church" is the "mother" of believers (sec. 4) as "God's people" and in whose school "we have been pupils all our lives." Outside the church we cannot hope for forgiveness of sin and Calvin warns that "it is always disastrous to leave the church." Through the humans who minister in the church, the church preaches and teaches. It worships God since "believers have no greater help than public worship, for by it God raises his own folk upward step by step" (sec. 5).

Calvin says Scripture refers to the church in two ways. The "invisible church" is composed of the children of God "by grace of adoption" who are "true members of Christ by sanctification of the Holy Spirit" (sec. 7). This church includes "not only the saints presently living on earth, but all the elect from the beginning of the world." Second, the "visible church" is the church throughout the world of those who "profess to worship one God and Christ." Those in the visible church participate in the sacraments. But in this church are "mingled many hypocrites who have nothing of Christ but the name and outward appearance. There are very many ambitious, greedy, envious persons, evil speakers and some of quite unclean life." Not all who confess Jesus Christ are genuine in their confession.

The invisible church is invisible to us but known by God. The visible church is known by us and God, but is a mixed body of true believers and those who make only an outward profession of faith. Calvin quoted Augustine to say that "many sheep are without, and many wolves are within" the church (sec. 8). But it is not for us to judge who is "out" and who is "in." All judgment belongs to God (2 Tim 2:19). We are to exercise a "charitable judgment" on others in the church, recognizing as Christians those who confess their faith, participate in the church, and live professing "the same God and Christ with us."

There are two marks of the church. Calvin wrote: "Wherever we see the Word of God purely preached and heard, and the sacraments administered according to Christ's institution, there, it is not to be doubted, a church of God exists [cf. Eph 2:20]" (sec. 9). These marks of the church express the nature of the church universal, which is "a multitude gathered from all nations; it is divided and dispersed in separate places, but agrees on the one truth of divine doctrine, and is bound by the bond of the same religion." Separation from the church, Calvin maintained, is "the denial of God and Christ" (sec. 10). There is no "perfect" church—because there are no "perfect Christians." Even when scandals emerge, the Lord requires "kindness" and not judging with "immoderate severity" (sec. 13). We are to continue in the church until the Day of Judgment." The church is "holy" in the sense that "it is daily advancing and is not yet perfect: it makes progress from day to day but has not yet reached its goal of holiness" (sec. 17). Like all in the church, we must seek forgiveness of sins, without which there is no church. By "God's generosity, mediated by

Christ's merit, through the sanctification of the Spirit, sins have been and are daily pardoned to us who have been received and engrafted into the body of the church" (sec. 21).

God uses humans to carry out the ministry of the church. Those who minister do not take over God's authority, for this is a "delegated work." "Through their mouths," God may "do his own work—just as a workman uses a tool to do his work" (4.3.1). God entrusts to humans "the teaching of salvation and everlasting life in order that through their hands it might be communicated to the rest." Human ministry, through which God governs the church, is the "chief sinew by which believers are held together in one body" (sec. 2).

There are offices of ministry in the church, drawn from Ephesians 4:11. These are apostles, prophets, evangelists, pastors, and teachers. The "care of the poor was entrusted to the deacons" (4.3.9) in the early church and in Calvin's Geneva, the deacons had an important role in providing relief for the poor and carrying out social ministries in the church. "All things should be done decently and in order" (1 Cor 14:40) in the church and the church's government should be carried out through orderly calling throughout the church (sec. 10). In the outer call of the church, pastors, teachers, and deacons are to be ordained by the "laying on of hands," a rite derived from Hebrew custom and used by the apostles in the early church. It signifies the offering to God of the new minister and to conferring of "the visible graces of the Spirit [Acts 19:6] to the one called to ministry" (sec. 16). Calvin mentions here the "presbytery," which evolved into the "Presbyterian" form of church government, practiced by descendants of Calvin in the Reformed tradition.

Calvin spends time discussing the ancient church and its government; the Papacy with its claims and growth; and how the Roman Catholic Church became corrupt (4.4–8).

He goes on to consider Councils and their authority (4.9); church constitutions (4.10); and the jurisdiction of the church and its abuse as seen in the Papacy (4.11). All these are windows into the issues at stake in Calvin's view between the Roman Church, and its theological views, and his own.

When Calvin discusses the discipline of the church, he sees it as necessary for the life of the church to call those who do not believe or live in accord with the gospel to repentance (4.12). Calvin urges a "rule of moderation" in contrast, at points to the "excessive severity of the ancients" (4.12.8). Excommunication is the ultimate form of church discipline. Yet, for the excommunicated, there is the hope that "they may turn to a more virtuous life and may return to the society and unity of the church" (sec. 10). Calvin warned: "Unless this gentleness is maintained in both private and public censures, there is danger lest we soon slide down from discipline to butchery."

SACRAMENTS (4.14)

Along with the preaching of the Word, the sacraments are crucial to the life of the church. They are God's gifts to aid our faith. Calvin proposes two definitions, either of which is acceptable. The first is that a sacrament is "an outward sign by which the Lord seals on our consciences the promises of his good will toward us in order to sustain the weakness of our faith; and we in turn attest our piety toward him in the presence of the Lord and of his angels and before men" (4.14.1). Sacraments are "signs" and "seals." They are expressions of God's "good will" to us and help sustain us in faith. By participating in sacraments, persons attest their piety before God and all people.

Sacraments are always to be accompanied by the Word (sec. 3). They are visible expressions or an outward sign of an inward grace (Augustine). The Word to which Calvin refers is the Word of God in preaching. Preaching proclaims God's promises. Preaching should "make us understand what the visible sign means" (sec. 4).

The sacraments are also seals. In ancient times, seals were attached to government documents. They are nothing in themselves but, when added to the writing, the seals confirm and seal what is written with the authority they represent. In the Old Testament, Abraham was given the sign of circumcision which was also a "seal" (Rom 4:11). Circumcision did not establish Abraham's justification. Circumcision was its sign. Circumcision "sealed" the covenant of faith "in which he had already been justified" (sec. 5). When Christian believers see sacraments, they rise up "in devout contemplation to those lofty mysteries which lie hidden in the sacraments."

Sacraments are "a visible word," God's promises "as painted in a picture" (Augustine; sec. 6). One "might call them mirrors," said Calvin, "in which we may contemplate the riches of God's grace, which he lavishes upon us." Through them, God "attests his good will and love toward us more expressly than by word." It is the Holy Spirit, "that inward teacher," who confirms and increases faith through the sacraments" (sec. 9). "If the Spirit be lacking," Calvin wrote, "the sacraments can accomplish nothing more in our minds than the splendor of the sun shining upon blind eyes, or a voice sounding in deaf ears." It is the Spirit in our hearts, "which is to conceive, sustain, nourish, and establish faith" and "the sacraments profit not a whit without the power of the Holy Spirit." To those already taught by the Spirit, the sacraments strengthen and enlarge faith in our hearts.

The sacraments work in conjunction with the Word of God. The apostle Paul experienced this, as if "the power of the Holy Spirit were joined by an indissoluble bond to his preaching for the inward illumination and moving of the mind" (sec. 11; see 1 Cor 2:4; 2 Cor 3:6). Both preaching and the sacraments are used by God's Spirit to confirm our faith. The Word of God in preaching brings faith because "faith comes from what is heard, and what is heard comes through the word of Christ" (Rom 10:17). Likewise, God "nourishes faith spiritually through the sacraments, whose one function is to set his promises before our eyes to be looked upon, indeed, to be guarantees of them to us" (sec. 12). Indeed, "the sacraments have the same office as the Word of God: to offer and set forth Christ to us, and in him the treasures of heavenly grace" (sec. 17).

BAPTISM (4.15–16)

Calvin recognizes two sacraments: Baptism and the Lord's Supper. Both of these are examples of God's accommodation—giving visible signs—adjusting to human capacities to provide symbols as "aids to true piety" (4.14.19).

Baptism for Calvin is "the sign of the initiation by which we are received into the society of the church, in order that, engrafted in Christ, we may be reckoned among God's children" (4.15.1). It is our entrance into the church, symbolized in some churches today by a baptismal font at the entrance to the sanctuary. Calvin invoked the image of the seal again when he wrote that "baptism should be a token and proof of our cleansing; or (the better to explain what I mean) it is like a sealed document to confirm to us that all our sins are so abolished, remitted, and effaced that they can never come to his sight." Baptism expresses the forgiveness of sin, giving a divine ratification that sin that is forgiven is also "forgotten" by God and does not have a continuing power in the life of a baptized Christian.

Book IV

The water of baptism does not contain the power to "cleanse, regenerate, and renew," nor is it the cause of salvation (sec.2). But in the sacrament is "received the knowledge and certainty of such gifts." The power of baptism is ongoing. It is a once-and-for-all event; we are "once for all washed and purged for our whole life" (sec. 3). But despite sins in the future, the effect of baptism continues: "For, though baptism, administered only once, seemed to have passed, it was still not destroyed by subsequent sins." For it is "Christ's purity" that has been given in baptism and "his purity ever flourishes; it is defiled by no spots, but buries and cleanses away all our defilements." This is a word of hope and courage for Christian living, even as Christians struggle with ongoing temptations and sin. Martin Luther often turned away from temptation by exclaiming, "I have been baptized." This carried out Calvin's comment about a function of baptism: "This doctrine is only given to sinners who groan, wearied and oppressed by their own sins, in order that they may have something to lift them up and comfort them, so as not to plunge into confusion and despair" (see also sec. 4).

Baptism is a token of our death to the power of sin (mortification) and our renewal in Christ (vivification), said Calvin (sec. 5). It also represents our union with Christ in that we become "so united to Christ himself that we become sharers in all his blessings" (sec. 6). This establishes the firmest possible bond for life. Baptism acknowledges the greatest blessing; for "all the gifts of God proferred in baptism are found in Christ alone." Baptism is a sign and seal of Jesus Christ himself.

Sacraments enable us to "see spiritual things in physical, as if set before our very eyes" (sec. 14). In baptism, the Lord, by "this token attests his will toward us, namely, that he is pleased to lavish all these things upon us. And he does not feed our eyes with a mere appearance only, but leads us to the present reality and effectively performs what it symbolizes." This is a key point for Calvin, who says a similar thing about the sacrament of the Lord's Supper (4.17.3). Against other Protestant Reformers, notably Huldrych Zwingli, who took the view that sacraments are primarily memorials to "remind us" of realities, Calvin believed that we do not just receive "a mere appearance" but that baptism "effectively performs what it symbolizes." God's grace in baptism is not merely "remembered," it is "received." The reality and the truth are joined to the sign, received in faith (sec. 15). Baptism confirms faith.

Calvin argues for the propriety and effectiveness of infant baptism. Adult baptism (called by some Anabaptist reformers, "Believer's Baptism") is found in the New Testament. The Anabaptists argued that, because there were no instances of babies being baptized in the New Testament, it is not a legitimate practice (see 4.16.1). But Calvin appeals to the Old Testament practice of circumcision (4.16.3). Circumcision was commanded by God to Abraham to be a sign of the covenant promise God made, that God would be God to Abraham and his descendants (Gen 17:7, 10). Later, God covenants with Abraham that he should live in uprightness and obedience (Gen 17:1).

For Calvin, Old Testament circumcision stands in an "anagogic" or "spiritual relationship" with New Testament baptism (4.16.4). This means that just as circumcision was a sign and seal of God's covenant with Abraham—promising to be his God and commanding him to live in obedience—so baptism is now a sign and seal of God's promise in Jesus Christ. God's covenant with Abraham, as "the first access to God" and "first entry into immortal life, is the forgiveness of sins." Accordingly, said Calvin, "this corresponds to the promise of baptism that we shall be cleansed." The command by God for Abraham to live in obedience "applies to mortification, or regeneration." The differences between circumcision and baptism lie only in the externals, in the visible ceremonies. But, "whatever belongs to circumcision pertains likewise to baptism." In summary: "Circumcision was for the Jews their first entry into the church, because it was a token to them by which they were assured of adoption as the people and household of God, and they in turn professed to enlist in God's service. In like manner, we also are consecrated to God through baptism, to be reckoned as his people, and in turn we swear fealty to him. By this it appears incontrovertible that baptism has taken the place of circumcision to fulfill the same office among us."

From this, Calvin sees that infants are participants in the covenant and that "baptism is properly administered to infants as something owed to them" (sec. 5). In the Old Testament, tiny infants received circumcision and thus participated "in all those things which were then signified by circumcision [cf. Gen 17:12]." This meant infants received the seal of "the promise of the covenant." If, "immediately after making the covenant with Abraham," God "commanded it to be sealed in infants by an outward sacrament [Gen 17:12], what excuse will Christians give for not testifying and sealing it in their children today?" (sec. 6). The covenant God made with Abraham "still holds good," says Calvin. Only "the manner of confirmation is different—what was circumcision for them [the Jews] was replaced for us by baptism."

Additionally, Calvin continued to write about Jesus who welcomed and blessed the little children (Matt 19:13–15). Calvin said about this: Jesus "attests his will by his act when, embracing them, he commends them with his prayer and blessing to his Father. If it is right for infants to be brought to Christ, why not also to be received into baptism, the symbol of our communion and fellowship with Christ?" (sec. 7).

Calvin saw infant baptism as children being received through "a solemn symbol of adoption before they were old enough to recognize him as Father" (sec. 9). What better symbol of the gift of salvation itself than an infant being adopted into the family of God, the church, in all its helplessness (see Rom 5:8)? This is pure salvation by grace.

LORD'S SUPPER (4.17–19)

Baptism is "an entrance and a sort of initiation into the church" (sec. 30). The Lord's Supper is "a spiritual banquet wherein Christ attests himself to be the life-giving bread, upon which our souls feed unto true and blessed immortality [John 6:51]" (4.17.1). The Supper nourishes us "throughout the course of our life."

In the Supper, "the signs are bread and wine, which represent for us the invisible food that we receive from the flesh and blood of God. For as in baptism, God, regenerating us, engrafts us into the society of his church and makes us his own by adoption, so as we have said, that he discharges the function of a provident householder in continually supplying to us the food to sustain and preserve us in that life into which he has begotten us by his Word." Christ is "the only food of our soul."

Like baptism, in the Lord's Supper, God has disclosed a divine mystery—"Christ's secret union with the devout," which is incomprehensible—through a "figure and image in visible signs best adapted to our small capacity." This accommodation to our needs shows that "just as bread and wine sustain physical life, so are souls fed by Christ." This is a "mystical blessing," confirming that "the Lord's body was once for all so sacrificed for us that we may now feed upon it, and by feeding feel in ourselves the working of that unique sacrifice." This sacrament brings "godly souls" a "great assurance and delight" because "they have a witness of our growth into one body with Christ such that whatever is his may be called ours," including eternal life (sec. 2). Christ has taken our sins upon himself so that "we cannot be condemned for our sins, from whose guilt he has absolved us, since he willed to take them upon himself as if they were his own." Calvin sees this as "the wonderful exchange" which, he says,

> out of his measureless benevolence, he has made with us; that, becoming Son of man with us, he has made us sons of God with him; that, by his descent to earth, he has prepared an ascent to heaven for us; that, by taking on our mortality, he has conferred his immortality upon us; that, accepting our weakness, he has strengthened us by his power; that, receiving our poverty unto himself, he has transferred his wealth to us; that, taking the weight of our iniquity upon himself (which oppressed us), he has clothed us with his righteousness. (sec. 2)

In the Lord's Supper, when Jesus said, "Take, eat, drink: this is my body, which is given for you; this is my blood, which is shed for forgiveness of sins" [Matt 26:26–28, conflated with 1 Cor 11:24; cf. Mark 14:22–24; Luke 22:19–20], Calvin said, "By bidding us take, he indicates that it is ours; by bidding us eat, that it is made one substance with us; by declaring that his body is given for us and his blood shed for us, he teaches that both are not so much his as ours. For he took up and laid down both, not for his own advantage but for our salvation." For Calvin, the "almost entire force of the Sacrament lies in these words: 'which is given for you,' 'which is shed for you'" (sec. 3).

The movement in the Lord's Supper is from the physical to the spiritual. As Calvin put it:

> From the physical things set forth in the Sacrament we are led by a sort of analogy to spiritual things. Thus, when bread is given as a symbol of Christ's body, we must at once grasp this comparison: as bread nourishes, sustains, and keeps the life of our body, so Christ's body is the only food to invigorate and enliven our soul. When we see wine set forth as a symbol of blood, we must reflect on the benefits which wine imparts to the body, and so realize that the same are spiritually imparted to us by Christ's blood. These benefits are to nourish, refresh, strengthen, and gladden (sec. 3).

The bread and wine are the outward elements whereby the spiritual presence of Jesus Christ is communicated. The Supper "sends us to the cross of Christ" where the promise of eternal life is found in the one whose flesh and blood "feed us unto eternal life" (see John 6:55, 56; sec. 4). We experience the benefits of his death. This happens by faith. In the sacred Supper, Jesus Christ "offers himself with all his benefits to us, and we receive him by faith" (sec. 5). Christ "seals such giving of himself by the sacred mystery of the Supper," when he "inwardly fulfills what he outwardly designates." In the Supper, "we eat Christ's flesh in believing, because it is made ours by faith . . . and this eating is the result and effect of faith." Faith is the means by which the benefits of Christ's death on the cross—salvation—is received by those who believe in him as they eat and drink in the Lord's Supper.

For Calvin it was important to maintain that the Holy Spirit's "secret power" is operative in the Supper as the Spirit "truly unites things separated in space" (sec. 10). The Holy

Spirit "fulfills what he promises" making Christ's promises of salvation effective. The power (Lat. *virtus*) of the Spirit to bring the benefits of promises to those who partake of the Supper by faith means that in the Lord's Supper, there is a true participation in Christ. The Supper "represents" Christ and "presents" Christ. Christ is present in the Supper. By faith, believers receive the benefits of all Christ has done. For Calvin, "The godly ought by all means to keep this rule: whenever they see symbols appointed by the Lord, to think and be persuaded that the truth of the thing signified is surely present there." Christ is present in the Supper with the symbols to communicate himself to believers in faith. Because "a visible sign is given us to seal the gift of a thing invisible, when we have received the symbol of the body, let us no less surely trust that the body itself is also given to us."

Calvin distinguished his view of the presence of Christ in the Supper from traditional Roman Catholicism, which taught transubstantiation (secs. 11–15). In this view, when the priest consecrates the bread and wine, the "substance" of those elements actually become the body and blood of Christ. Their outward appearance remains the same, they still look like bread and wine. But their inner reality or "substance" (as in Greek philosophy) is transformed, a "conversion of the bread into the body takes place," as Calvin puts it (sec. 14). Calvin maintained this view converts the bread into Christ and that this is opposed by "God's clear Word" (sec. 14). In the Roman view, in the phrase, "This *is* my body" the "is" would mean "to be transubstantiated."

Against Lutheran views, sometimes called "consubstantiation," in which Christ is held to be bodily present "with" and "under" the untransformed elements of the bread and wine (sec. 20), Calvin argued for the spiritual presence of Christ.

On the other end of the spectrum, the Zurich reformer, Huldrych Zwingli applied his view of "sacrament" to the Lord's Supper and said that in the phrase, "This *is* my body," the word "is" means "signifies" or "represents." It is a metaphor for believing in Christ. Christ's presence is only as believers have faith and remember him. The elements are only signs. They are not what the signs signify. For Zwingli, the key phrase was "Do this in remembrance of me" (Luke 22:19; 1 Cor 11:24).[1]

These differing theological positions about the presence of Christ in the Lord's Supper were to end up separating different branches of the Protestant Reformation. It is sadly ironic that the meal Jesus shared with his disciples, which is celebrated in the sacrament of the Lord's Supper and which should unite all Christian believers, has been such a serious source of division among believers.

Calvin believed the Lord's Supper should be celebrated frequently (secs. 44–46) and that both the bread and the wine should be distributed to all who participate in the communion (secs. 47–50). This was in opposition to the Roman Catholic practice of withholding the cup of wine from the laity. Calvin went on to describe the papal Mass as a sacrilege (4.18). Rome taught that at each celebration of the Mass, Christ was resacrificed on the cross so, said Calvin, "Christ ought to be sacrificed daily to be of any benefit to us" (4.18.7). Calvin believed that "there are no other sacrifices, but that this one [Christ] was offered only once and is never to be repeated" (sec. 3; cf. Heb 7:27; 9:12, 26; 10:2, 10). Calvin also maintained against the Roman view of seven sacraments, that Baptism and the Lord's Supper are the only true sacraments (4.18.19–20; 4.19).

Calvin recognized that theological speculation was involved, especially here with regard to technical questions

---

1. See McKim, *Theological Turning Points*, 142–50.

about the Lord's Supper. It was important to articulate theological views. But Calvin indicated on the question of the nature of Christ's presence in the Supper: "Now, if anyone should ask me how this takes place, I shall not be ashamed to confess that it is a secret too lofty for either my mind to comprehend or my words to declare. And, to speak more plainly, I rather experience than understand it" (4.17.32). In the end, the Lord's Supper is a sacrament for sinners who are united by faith with Jesus Christ. "For it is a sacrament," Calvin declared, "ordained not for the perfect, but for the weak and feeble, to awaken, arouse, stimulate, and exercise the feeling of faith and love, indeed to correct the defect of both" (4.17.42). This points Christian believers in the right directions.

CIVIL GOVERNMENT (4.20)

Calvin concluded his *Institutes* with a chapter on civil government. He believed humans were under a "twofold government" and because he had discussed the spiritual government of the inner person that "pertains to eternal life" (4.3–11), he turns to the other kind of government, which pertains to "the establishment of civil justice and outward morality" (4.20.1).

While some see earthly governments as unclean, beneath their own "excellence" to be concerned with, civil government does have its "appointed end." Calvin saw this as "to cherish and protect the outward worship of God, to defend sound doctrine of piety and the position of the church, to adjust our life to the society of men, to form our social behavior to civil righteousness, to reconcile us with one another, and to promote general peace and tranquility" (sec. 2). All these tasks are necessary in a society, as necessary Calvin says as "bread, water, sun, and air" (sec. 3). Striking to our ears is Calvin's firm conviction that a primary function of civil government is its duty of "rightly establishing religion." He dealt with civil government in three parts: "the magistrate, who is the protector and guardian of the laws; the laws, according to which he governs; the people, who are governed by the laws and obey the magistrate."

Calvin saw the office of the magistrate as very important. Magistrates, he believed, "have a mandate from God, have been invested with divine authority, and are wholly God's representatives, in a manner, acting as his vicegerents" (sec. 4). He cites a variety of biblical passages and examples to show that "princes are ministers of God, for those doing good unto praise; for those doing evil, avengers unto wrath [Rom 13:3-4]." The Lord approves of the office of magistrate, the question is whether the magistrate will be obedient to God, or not. But the work is important. As Calvin said, "no one ought to doubt that civil authority is a calling, not only holy and lawful before God, but also the most sacred and by far the most honorable of all callings in the whole life of mortal men." A calling—high praise for the magistrate!

Magistrates are to remember they are "vicars of God," who "have been ordained ministers of divine justice" (sec. 6). They are to live accordingly. They serve in "a most holy office, since they are serving as God's deputies."

There are diverse forms of government, each having its own usefulness. For Calvin: "I will not deny that aristocracy, or a system compounded of aristocracy and democracy, far excels all others" (sec. 8). This is primarily because there are checks and balances that help to counter human "willfulness" when a person tries to assert too much power. This was important because Calvin recognized the natural sinfulness of all persons.

Magistrates who exercise rule are to be concerned with both tables of the law of God—honoring God by supporting religion; and the execution of human justice (sec. 9). Justice is "to receive into safekeeping, to embrace, to protect, vindicate, and free the innocent." The judgment that must be meted out is "to withstand the boldness of the impious, to repress their violence, to punish their misdeeds. This can require force, which magistrates should administer" (sec. 10). In the teachings of Scripture, when punishment is carried out, the magistrate is doing not his own work but God's. The magistrate must not veer to the boundaries: neither "abrupt and savage harshness" nor complete laxness. Clemency is needed (which Seneca had called "the chief gift of princes"). The magistrate must find the way to rule that honors God.

Relatedly, Calvin saw governments as having the right to wage war. Kings and people must sometimes wage war to execute "public vengeance" (sec. 11). Political leaders must protect the lands over which they have responsibilities. Both "natural equity and the nature of the office dictate that princes must be armed not only to restrain the misdeeds of private individuals by judicial punishment, but also to defend by war the dominions entrusted to their safekeeping, if at any time they are under enemy attack." The Holy Spirit, also, "declares such wars to be lawful by many testimonies of Scripture," a statement directed against the pacifism of the Anabaptists. Yet there must be restraint and humanity in war. Magistrates must guard against "giving vent to their passions even in the slightest degree" (sec. 12).

Calvin believed Christians are free to use law courts and means of litigation, but again, without hatred and revenge (sec. 17). Some (especially the Anabaptists), believed there should be no participation in the legal system because it is forbidden by the New Testament. But, says Calvin, the magistrate is "minister of God for our good [Rom 13:4]," to protect and help people live "a quiet and serene life [1 Tim 2:2]." On the other hand, there are those who are overly litigious and who "boil with a rage for litigation," fueled by "bitter and deadly hatred, and an instance passion to revenge and hurt." So while going to law is permitted, it cannot be when one has hatred toward another or because of being "seized with a mad desire to harm another or hound him relentlessly" (cf. secs. 18–21).

In the case of unjust rulers, Christians must first "think most honorably" toward the office of magistrates, as a "jurisdiction bestowed by God" (sec. 22). Willing obedience should be shown by things such as obeying proclamations, paying taxes, etc. Since the magistracy is to be obeyed (Rom 13:1–2; Titus 3:1; 1 Pet 2:13–14), the magistrate cannot be resisted "without God being resisted at the same time" (sec. 23). This adherence is due even to unjust magistrates (sec. 24) when it comes to public obedience (sec. 25). In the Scriptures, obedience was due even to bad kings (secs. 26–29). Sometimes God acts to "deliver his people, oppressed in unjust ways, from miserable calamity" (sec. 30). But as far as individuals are concerned, "if the correction of unbridled despotism is the Lord's to avenge, let us not at once think that it is entrusted to us, to whom no command has been given except to obey and suffer" (sec. 31).

However, Calvin does indicate that while these are prescriptions for "private individuals," if there are now "any magistrates of the people, appointed to restrain the willfulness of kings (as in ancient times the ephors were set against the Spartan kings, or the tribunes of the people against the Roman consuls, or the demarchs against the senate of the Athenians) . . . I am so far from forbidding them to withstand, in accordance with their duty, the fierce licentiousness of kings, that, if they wink at kings who violently fall upon and assault the lowly common folk, I declare that their dissimulation involves nefarious perfidy, because they dishonestly betray the freedom of the people, of which they know that they have been appointed protectors by God's ordinance." This statement, along with others Calvin made along the way, are often seen as opening the door to potential political resistance. In Calvin's later followers, notably John Knox, the note of resistance was magnified.[2]

The final section of Calvin's *Institutes* strongly asserts that obedience to earthly kings should never lead to disobedience to the Lord. This was the same emphasis he struck in his 1536 *Institutes*. Calvin wrote: "But in that obedience which we have shown to be due the authority of rulers, we are always to make this exception, indeed, to observe it as primary, that such obedience is never to lead us away from obedience to him, to whose will the desires of all kings ought to be subject, to whose decrees all their commands ought to yield, to whose majesty their scepters ought to be submitted" (sec. 32; cf. 2.8.38). For

> the Lord, therefore, is the King of Kings, who, when he has opened his sacred mouth, must alone be heard, before all and above all men; next to him we are subject to those men who are in authority over us, but only in him. If they command anything against him, let it go unesteemed. And here let us not be concerned about all that dignity which the magistrates possess; for no harm is done to it when it is humbled before that singular and truly supreme power of God. (sec. 32).

The words of the apostle Peter are the basis for this higher obedience, owed to God: "We must obey God rather than any human authority" (Acts 5:29). For Calvin, "let us

---

2. See note 54 in Calvin, *Institutes* 4.20.31; and Busch, "Church and Politics in the Reformed Tradition," 180–95.

comfort ourselves with the thought that we are rendering that obedience which the Lord requires when we suffer anything rather than turn aside from piety."

The final ascription in the *Institutes* expresses what for John Calvin was the supreme end of human life and of considering the knowledge of God and the knowledge of ourselves, the Knowledge of God the Creator and the Knowledge of God the Redeemer: GOD BE PRAISED.

DISCUSSION QUESTIONS

Life of Calvin

EARLY YEARS AND EDUCATION (1509–1536)

- What were important effects of Renaissance Humanism for Calvin's life as a theologian?
- What are the significant elements of Calvin's "sudden conversion" and what does his relative silence about it, say to us?
- What does Calvin's willingness to strike out in new directions as a "Protestant" say about the nature of his Christian faith?
- Why did Calvin feel it was important to write his 1536 *Institutes*?

CALLED TO GENEVA (1536–1538)

- What lessons did Calvin's difficulties in Geneva teach him?

STRASBOURG (1538–1541)

- In what ways did Calvin's ministries in Strasbourg prepare him for his future ministries in Geneva?

RETURN TO GENEVA (1541–1549)

- What do you imagine Calvin felt when he returned to Geneva?
- What benefits do you see in the way the Genevan church was organized?
- What were strengths and weaknesses in the organization of the Geneva city government?
- Why were worship and catechisms so important for the church in Geneva?
- In what ways would preaching, teaching, and learning shape the way Christian belief and life were experienced in Geneva?

THE GENEVAN CHURCH (1550–1555)

- In what ways do you imagine Calvin's study of the Bible helped him through the difficulties he faced in Geneva?
- Why were Calvin and the city of Geneva adamant against heretical views, such as held by Bolsec?
- Do you agree or disagree that the case of Servetus has left a permanent blemish on the reputation of Calvin?

FINAL YEARS (1556–1564)

- What aspects of Calvin's final days and death are most striking to you?

Theology of Calvin

BOOK ONE:
THE KNOWLEDGE OF GOD THE CREATOR

Knowing God and Knowing Ourselves (1.1–2)

- What are differences between an intellectual and a personal knowledge of God?
- Why is piety important in the study of theology for Calvin?

The Knowledge of God in Us (1.3–5)

- What evidences are there of an innate knowledge of God in humans?
- What evidences of humans' smothering or suppression of the knowledge of God do you see?

Another and Better Help: The Scriptures (1.6–9)

- In what way is the revelation of God in Scripture a "better help" than the revelation of God in creation?
- Why is it important that recognition of the authority of Scripture comes by the work of the Holy Spirit rather than from human reason?

God the Creator (1.10–12)

- Why is idolatry such a dangerous practice?
- In what ways is God's "accommodation" an important concept?

Trinity (1.13)

- Why did the early church believe it was important to confess the three persons of the Trinity are all equally God?
- Why did the early church believe it was important to confess that the one God is God in three persons?

Angels and Demons (1.14.1–19)

- What functions do angels carry out?
- Why is it important to affirm that demonic forces stand under the power of God?

Creator and Creation (1.14.20–22)

- In what ways do we experience the goodness of God's creation?
- Why does God's good creation evoke love and service to God?

Human Nature (1.15)

- In what ways does Calvin's description of human nature ring true in your experience?
- Why is the image of Jesus Christ as the Second Adam appropriate to deal with human nature?

Providence (1.16–18)

- What are ways in which God's providence is experienced?
- In what ways is the doctrine of providence a comforting doctrine?

BOOK II:
THE KNOWLEDGE OF GOD THE REDEEMER IN CHRIST

Knowledge of Ourselves (2.1–3)

- What is the theological importance of affirming humanity's basic dependence on God?
- What is the source of the knowledge of ourselves?

The Ruin of the Race (2.1.4–7)

- What are examples of the results of human sin?
- In what sense does each person share in the sin of Adam?

Original Sin (2.1.8–11)

- In what ways does original sin affect human life?
- Is it possible for any dimensions of life to be unaffected by original sin?

Corruption of the Will (2.2)

- Why do people resist the idea that the human will is unfree to accept the good of God?

- Why does the corruption of the will show the need for the work of the Holy Spirit?

Conversion of the Corrupt Will (2.3–5)

- In what ways does the corruption of the human will magnify the grace of God?
- What is the relation between the corruption of the human will by sin and the new creation God gives in Jesus Christ?

Redemption in Christ (2.6)

- Why is it necessary for Jesus Christ to be the one to bring redemption from human sin?
- Why is Jesus Christ the supreme example of God's accommodation to human capacities?

The Law of God (2.7–8)

- What are ways in which the law as a guide for Christian life (third function of the law) is important today?
- What do you think of Calvin's view that, besides the prohibitions in the Ten Commandments, there are also prescriptions for positive actions?

Old and New Testaments (2.9–11)

- In what ways did Calvin see "covenant" as being significant?
- Why was it important for Calvin to stress the continuities between the Old and New Testaments?

Discussion Questions

Jesus Christ the Mediator (2.12–15)

- Why is it important that Jesus Christ be both truly divine and truly human?
- In what ways are Jesus Christ as prophet, king, and priest helpful images for describing the work of Christ?

Jesus Christ the Redeemer (2.16.1–12; 2.17)

- Why was it necessary that it be Jesus Christ who is the Redeemer?
- Why was it important for Jesus Christ to be obedient to God in order to secure redemption?

Jesus Christ's Resurrection, Ascension, and Heavenly Intercession (2.16.13–18)

- Why is the resurrection of Jesus Christ so central to Christian faith?
- What are the benefits of Christ's resurrection?

BOOK III:
THE WAY IN WHICH WE RECEIVE THE GRACE OF CHRIST: WHAT BENEFITS COME TO US FROM IT, AND WHAT EFFECTS FOLLOW

The Work of the Holy Spirit (3.1)

- What benefits comes from the work of the Holy Spirit?
- Why is it important that faith originates by the Holy Spirit?

Faith (3.2)

- What elements are found in Calvin's understanding of faith?
- Why is faith as a relationship of trust and union with Christ able to sustain Christian life through all circumstances?

Repentance (3.3–5)

- What is the difference between seeing repentance as a step toward faith compared to repentance as an expression of faith?
- Why is it important for Christians to realize that even in faith, they will never be "perfect"?

The Christian Life (3.6–10)

- In what ways is self-denial "the sum of the Christian life"?
- What resources help Christians to "bear the cross" in their lives?

Justification (3.11–18)

- Why are the two elements of justification: forgiveness of sins and imputation of Christ's righteousness so important in justification?
- What does the phrase "justification by faith" mean?

Christian Freedom (3.19)

- In what ways are you aware of exercising Christian freedom?

- What effects would it have if Christians saw more practices as being "things indifferent"?

Prayer (3.20)

- In what ways does the practice of prayer shape Christian life?
- Are there "unanswered prayers"?

Election and Predestination (3.21–24)

- In what ways does the doctrine of election show that salvation is by God's grace?
- Why is Jesus Christ as the "mirror" of election an important theological and practical image?

The Final Resurrection (3.25)

- What reactions do you have to the expression of Christ desiring to "have us as companions in the life to come"?
- Why is hope for our future resurrection grounded in the resurrection of Jesus Christ?

BOOK IV:
THE EXTERNAL MEANS OR AIDS BY WHICH GOD INVITES US INTO THE SOCIETY OF CHRIST AND HOLDS US THERE

The Church (4.1–13)

- In what ways is it helpful to think of the "visible" and the "invisible" church?

- Why is participation in the visible church a key expression of Christian faith?

Sacraments (4.14)

- Why are sacraments important?
- In what ways are the images of sacraments as "signs" and "seals" important?

Baptism (4.15–16)

- Why is it significant that baptism be seen as having an effect one's whole life long?
- What images of baptism are particularly important in Calvin's thought?

Lord's Supper (4.17–19)

- In what ways does the Lord's Supper nourish the Christian life?
- Do you agree with Calvin's statement about the Lord's Supper that "I rather experience than understand it"?

Civil Government (4.20)

- In what ways do Calvin's views of civil government encourage Christians to participate in it?
- What are key insights of Calvin's view of civil government that are applicable to all particular forms or expressions of government?

SELECT BIBLIOGRAPHY

Battles, Ford Lewis. "God Was Accommodating Himself to Human Capacity," In *Readings in Calvin's Theology*, edited by Donald K. McKim, 21–42. Eugene, OR: Wipf and Stock, 1998.

Battles, Ford Lewis, trans. and ed. *The Piety of John Calvin: A Collection of His Spiritual Prose, Poems, and Hymns*. Phillipsburg, NJ: P. & R., 2009.

Battles, Ford Lewis, assisted by John R. Walchenbach. *Analysis of the Institutes of the Christian Religion of John Calvin*. Phillipsburg, NJ: P. & R., 2001.

Battles, Ford Lewis, and André Malan Hugo. *Calvin's Commentary on Seneca's "De Clementia" with Introduction, Translation, and Notes*. Leiden: Brill, 1969.

Beza, Theodore. *The Life of John Calvin*. Translated by Henry Beveridge. Philadelphia: Westminster, 1909.

Bouwsma, William J. *John Calvin: A Sixteenth Century Portrait*. New York: Oxford University Press, 1988.

Busch, Eberhard. "Church and Politics in the Reformed Tradition." In *Major Themes in the Reformed Tradition*, edited by Donald K. McKim, 180–95. Eugene, OR: Wipf and Stock, 1998.

Calvin: Institutes of the Christian Religion. CD. http://www.wjkbooks.com/Products/0664231705/calvin-individual-use-license.aspx

Calvin, John. *Calvin's Institutes: Abridged Edition*. Edited by Donald K. McKim. Louisville: Westminster John Knox, 2001.

———. *The Epistles of Paul The Apostle to the Romans and to the Thessalonians*. 12 vols. Edited by David W. Torrance and Thomas F. Torrance. Translated by Ross Mackenzie. Calvin's New Testament Commentaries. Grand Rapids: Eerdmans, 1961.

———. *Institutes of the Christian Religion*. 2 vols. Edited by John T. McNeill. Translated by Ford Lewis Battles. LCC 20–21. Philadelphia: Westminster, 1960.

Select Bibliography

———. *Institutes of the Christian Religion: 1536 Institutes.* Translated and annotated by Ford Lewis Battles. Grand Rapids: Eerdmans, 1975.

———. *Institutes of the Christian Religion: 1541 French Edition.* Translated by Elsie Anne McKee. Grand Rapids: Eerdmans, 2009.

———. *Instruction in Faith (1537).* Translated and edited by Paul T. Fuhrmann. Louisville, KY: Westminster John Knox, 1992.

———. Preface to *Commentary on Psalms.* 5 vols. Translated by James Anderson. Calvin Translation Society. Edinburgh, 1845.

Calvin: Theological Treatises. Edited by J. K. S. Reid. LCC. Philadelphia: Westminster, 1954.

Calvini Opera Database 1.0. Edited by Herman J. Selderhuis. Apeldoorn: Instituut voor Reformatieonderzoek, 2005. DVD.

Calvinism Research Database. http://www.calvin.edu/library/database/card/

Christian Classics Ethereal Library. http://www.ccel.org/

Cooke, Charles. "Calvin's Illnesses and Their Relation to Christian Vocation." In *Calvin Studies IV*, edited by John Leith and W. Stacy Johnson, 41–52. Davidson, NC: Davidson College, 1988.

Cottret, Bernard. *Calvin: A Biography.* Translated by M. Wallace McDonald. Grand Rapids: Eerdmans, 2000.

Davis, Thomas J. *John Calvin.* Spiritual Leaders and Thinkers. Philadelphia: Chelsea House, 2005.

De Greef, Wulfert. *The Writings of John Calvin, Expanded Edition: An Introductory Guide.* Translated by Lyle D. Bierma. Louisville: Westminster John Knox, 2008.

De Gruchy, John W. *John Calvin: Christian Humanist and Evangelical Reformer.* Eugene, OR: Wipf and Stock, 2013.

Elwood, Christopher. *Calvin for Armchair Theologians.* Illustrations by Ron Hill. Louisville: Westminster John Knox, 2002.

Ganoczy, Alexandre. *The Young Calvin.* Translated by David Foxgrover and Wade Provo. Philadelphia: Westminster, 1987.

Gordon, Bruce. *Calvin.* New Haven: Yale University Press, 2009.

H. Henry Meeter Center for Calvin Studies, The. Calvin College and Calvin Theological Seminary, Grand Rapids, Michigan. http://www.calvin.edu/meeter.

Hesselink, I. John. *Calvin's First Catechism: A Commentary, Featuring Ford Lewis Battles's Translation of the 1538 Catechism.* Columbia Series in Reformed Theology. Louisville: Westminster John Knox, 1997.

John Calvin Collection. Ages Digital Library. CD.

Select Bibliography

John Calvin: His Life & Legacy. DVD. Presbyterian Church (USA). http://www.wjkbooks.com/Products/9781571532053/john-calvin.aspx

John Calvin Bibliography, The. http://www.calvin.edu/meeter/publications/calvin-bibliography.htm

Johnson, William Stacy. *John Calvin: Reformer for the 21st Century*. Louisville: Westminster John Knox, 2009.

John Calvin: Catechism 1538. Translated and annotated by Ford Lewis Battles. Pittsburgh: Pittsburgh Theological Seminary, 1972.

Letters of John Calvin. 4 vols. Edited by Jules Bonnet. Philadelphia: Presbyterian Board of Publication, 1858.

McGrath, Alister E. *A Life of John Calvin: A Study in the Shaping of Western Culture*. Cambridge: Blackwell, 1990.

McKim, Donald K. *Coffee with Calvin: Daily Devotions*. Louisville: Westminster John Knox, 2013.

———. *Theological Turning Points*. Atlanta: John Knox, 1988.

McKim, Donald K., ed. *Calvin and the Bible*. New York: Cambridge University Press, 2006.

———. *The Cambridge Companion to John Calvin*. New York: Cambridge University Press, 2004.

———. *Readings in Calvin's Theology*. Eugene, OR: Wipf and Stock, 1998.

Parker, T. H. L. *John Calvin: A Biography*. 1975. Reprint, Louisville: Westminster John Knox, 2006.

———. *Portrait of Calvin*. Philadelphia: Westminster, 1961.

Partee, Charles. *The Theology of John Calvin*. Louisville: Westminster John Knox, 2008.

Post-Reformation Digital Library. http://www.prdl.org

Rogers, Jack B. and Donald K. McKim. *The Authority and Interpretation of the Bible: An Historical Approach*. Eugene, OR: Wipf and Stock, 1999.

Selderhuis, Herman J. *John Calvin: A Pilgrim's Life*. Translated by Albert Gootjes. Downer's Grove, IL: InterVarsity, 2009.

Selderhuis, Herman J., ed. *The Calvin Handbook*. Grand Rapids: Eerdmans, 2009.

Stroup, George W. *Calvin*. Abingdon Pillars of Theology. Nashville: Abingdon, 2009.

van't Spijker, Willem. *Calvin: A Brief Guide to His Life and Thought*. Translated by Lyle D. Bierma. Louisville: Westminster John Knox, 2009.

Walker, Willison. *John Calvin: Organiser of Reformed Protestantism. 1509–1564*. 1906. Reprint, New York: Schocken, 1969.

Select Bibliography

Wendel, François. *Calvin: The Origins and Development of His Religious Thought*. Translated by Philip Mairet. 1963. Reprint, London: Collins, 1965.

Works by John Calvin in English. http://www.calvin.edu/meeter/calvin-works-in-english/

www.ingramcontent.com/pod-product-compliance
Lightning Source LLC
Chambersburg PA
CBHW032158160426
43197CB00008B/966